ACKNOWLEDGEMENTS

I was overwhelmed, honoured, and excited to be asked to write this book. Then imposter thinking told me, on many occasions, that I wasn't really good enough to do this. It has been a long personal process of writing this book because there is so much research in this field that even I have been swaying between opinions, facts, and confusing figures over the last few years. I became overwhelmed lots of times and wondered how I could translate this for the audience when I was feeling stuck. The imposter gremlin wanted feeding after midnight so often and I admit this was the hardest book to write so far.

Sadly, I made a mistake in my first attempts at writing and did not do my due diligence, homework, or research as well as I could and should have done at the time. I bought into a quick fix because it matched my cognitive and attributional biases. A human error that I am hoping to rectify here. This error was driven by the want to protect and advocate, for children and young people, because I was angry at the high and increasing rates of pathologising children with technology-related 'disorders' (and the cost to parents and the fear-mongering that has arisen in this space). I wanted to write a balanced book and in doing so have spent so many hours reading works that are written with such passion, and sometimes with blind spots about their own reasoning. I hope that I am doing the inner work (of healing and growth), personally as well as a scholar. It is tiring but fruitful work.

I deemed it very important that I show the balanced space of research and findings about these topics and not weigh you down with endless references so you can read an unfolding story of reason and make up your own mind.

I hope I have written a book you find helpful, and it meets your expectations of managing your social media and gaming habits.

Cath

WHO AM I AND WHY AM I GIVING YOU THIS ADVICE?

Cath is a human being, a mum to two now fully grown men in their twenties. Her introduction to Computers began before she had reached the age of ten as her father saw this as the new world and he was correct. She introduced her boys to the world of computing and technology when they were as young as three, because she knew this was going to move fast and wanted them skilled in what would be their future.

Cath's primary job role on leaving schooling was a REME Electrical, Mechanical and Electronic Engineer: Instruments (optronics) in the Army. She was the first woman ever to complete the training for this role. She fixed day and night sights (tanks and other armoured vehicles), thermal observations sights, tank laser sights and their power supply systems and some other stuff like theodolites (great times). When she left the Army, she went to work in what was called IT and Early Cybersecurity/Data protection taking up first and third line roles which included working with casinos, petrol stations, banks, Dell, Siemens, Hewlett Packard and more.

She decided to take up counselling and psychotherapy in the evenings as her boys were growing and went on to complete her BSc (Hons) at Huddersfield University with her dissertation looking at eye tracking around double negatives (spurred on by online terms

DOI: 10.4324/9781032617251-1

and conditions about IT services). As her boys were still in school Cath went back into the gaming world working for a company (SponG) with EA, Nintendo, Activision, Blizzard, and other companies. As she was working she trained monthly on a weekend over four years to become a dual adult and child psychotherapist. She also worked as a relationship and sexual education tutor in primary and secondary schools when she first realised that cybertrauma was an issue in 2011. She is also a clinical supervisor.

Excited by study once more Cath went on to complete both the adult and child psychotherapy MSc (at the same time) at Newman University and gained her UCKP accredited status after completing 1,200 supervised hours. She is still studying and will have likely completed her PhD by the time of publication in cybertrauma (and how this impacts young children).

Cath runs her own company providing clinical supervision, trauma psychotherapy for children and adults, consultancy, training and keynotes on online harm and cybertrauma. She runs courses on cybertrauma, the impact on children of viewing adult sexual material, child sexual abuse material online and victim impact, and works with large national and international (statutory and voluntary) organisations supporting professionals in the field of cybertrauma (viewing this for their role) and how to manage burnout.

Cath is the lead for the Digital Harms and Impact stream in the West Yorkshire Adversity, Trauma and Resilience framework ensuring West Yorkshire Trauma is informed by 2030 and run by the Integrated Care Board and Violence Reduction Unit. She is also a member of the other streams (education, policing, health, suicide prevention, and the steering group given her knowledge of trauma and technology together).

Cath is also a Functional Health Practitioner (BANT) and holds a qualification in DNA Health Testing with Nordic Laboratories, where she works with some patients to assess their bodies functionality and provide nutrigenomic care.

She works with a global organisation around virtual reality for mental health (MHVR), and global organisations regarding newer emerging technologies (XRSI), Scenegraph Studios who created Spirit VR, Get Safe Online, Online Safety UK, Marie Collins, (NCPS), Counselling Tutor and Nscience for Psychotherapy, Gamers Beat Cancer and other companies who cannot be named at this time for legally binding reasons.

She educates therapists, psychologists, and other professionals about data protection and cybersecurity in SMEs about how they can protect their clients' and patients' data in a world of technology. This has included some peer reviewed research for *Frontiers in Psychology* and *Politics International*.

From 2022 Cath has been writing for Routledge Psychology and has produced four books (five with this one!) in just over two years. She gave a TEDx talk in October 2022 at Doncaster on Bodies, Brains, and Technology: the real social dilemma (Knibbs, 2022). She has written chapters on Compassion in Cyberspace (Knibbs, 2020), Online Harm, Online Living and the impact for children and young people (Knibbs, 2021), and Ethics and Cyberethics (Knibbs, 2023) for a white paper about the use of VR in therapy (in press) and has several chapters due out in 2024.

In 2023 Cath won a national award, The Real Cyber Impact, for her 'determined and impactful' work in this field. She was also a winner in the top 50 women in computing.

Cath has much more to write in this field and fields that overlap. Technology is not going away, and neither is her advocacy and passion.

1

HOW DOES TECHNOLOGY INFLUENCE US AND WHAT DOES THE RESEARCH SAY?

WHAT PROMETHEUS TAUGHT US?

If you have a curious mind or listen to stories or watch films, you may have heard of the Greek god *Prometheus* (not the Alien Franchise film in this case). It is said he stole fire from the gods and gave it to humans and for this was tortured for all eternity (a bit much if you ask me, but gods really know how to enforce the wrath and smiting for sure!) and so perhaps we overly honour this technology for everything it can and does give us. But like fire ultimately how we progress as a species and utilise its power will determine our fate.

Fire was not our first technology, but we often look to this as the giver and taker of life enabling us to cook (softer foods for our palette) and bring us light when the sun sets, way before the invention of electricity and filament bulbs. As we mastered fire, the production of new and further tools was made possible (by mixing and melting metals and or chemicals) and fire is still one of the most important elements of our lives to date.

But what is 'technology' when I write about it here in this book and why do you even need to know about this concept as you are

DOI: 10.4324/9781032617251-2

reading about social media and gaming, and the understanding of how you use social media and gaming, and the impact this can have on your mental health? Why is this important?

TECHNE AND TECHNOLOGY: HOW THIS CHANGES US AND OUR BEHAVIOUR

There are as many ways to look at technology as there are disciplines that do so, such as computing, engineering, psychology, sociology, marketing, business, economics, and the health industries to name a few. It is likely that all around the world, some element of technology is in daily use for and within that geographical location. It's also used both similarly and differently in those locations. For example, there are not many Silicon Valley-type buildings in the Aboriginal communities I suspect, yet the technology created at Silicon Valley is most certainly in use in remote settings such as these.

Technology is the force of change for progress and also the facilitator, contributor, and tool with which our behaviour changes and we as a species utilise, embrace, and harness these tools, which the philosopher Heidegger (1977) referred to as 'techne'. This term was used to suggest that these tools are not a means to an end but an extension of our thinking and being. The technology becomes part of who we are and who we become and so the use of these social media and gaming spaces is indeed changing the way we 'operate' in the world and how those changes impact us over a longer period is not fully known.

What is both exciting and worrying is the speed at which we are moving through this technological revolution and Heidegger warns of the dangers of such technology progress, and at the time of submission of this writing, the introduction of Artificial Intelligence models into the world are already nearly a year old.

If we look at one of the seminal papers and approaches top this 'technology' we can see that the work of Kranzberg (1986) is still one of the most cited phrases by tech entrepreneurs; 'technology is neither good, nor bad, nor neutral' and this is reiterated by Hare (2022) in her book with a similar title. The ethics of this topic (including AI and cyberethics) leaves us with much work to do and I have much more to say on this (in chapters elsewhere) as they are complex issues and require depth of conversation from many in the space of tech, wellbeing, child safety, and policies.

COMPUTING TECHNOLOGIES

In this book, I am focusing the conversation on technology that is underpinned by computing as a paradigm and this means that I am really referring to the things that have evolved to be now called 'screens'. Perhaps those devices you hold in your hand, have in your house, and use to connect to the internet.

Before we get to the handheld and desktop devices that are so common in so many spaces that are part of your life, let us take a quick trip down memory lane to consider why this 'technology' is becoming so ubiquitous in our daily lives and how it is changing us.

The approach to technology is broad in its approach taking a broad, zoomed out **meta** lens (not the company formerly known as Facebook) but a wide-angle approach to the inclusion of this technology into our lives and how, let's say reliant we become on it. For example, fire has been replaced in some ways by electricity to cook food but is still the principle of energy behind the cooking of that food, which is not possible without heat.

To understand some of the influences, I will be referring to literature, some research, some common knowledge, some of my previous writings, and perhaps some films, videos, and podcasts so that you can understand the process, the subtle adaptations, and integrations of technology into your life and how you may no longer even notice this until it is pointed out. There are suggestions for further reading in the bibliography as I wanted to keep textual references minimal to enhance the readability of the book and ensure the flow of the conversation matches that of the real world.

For example, in my earlier books (Knibbs, 2022, 2023a, 2023b), I briefly discuss the kinds of terminology we use thanks to a researcher called Prensky (2001) to describe to those of us who are new to technology, known as *digital immigrants* and those who have grown up with it, *digital natives*. Now I talk about the kitchen (appliance) being native for example *the kettle native*, and why this language is unhelpful for those of us who have been working with computers for a long time (ahem!) who might present chronologically as an immigrant but are natives in the truest sense of this word.

And what terrible language this technology 'immigrant or native' is because it assumes a 'them and us' position and can inflect a hierarchy when there doesn't need to be one. This is often the language used by adults claiming they can't and don't understand technology, when we have phrases like silver surfer and technophobe too.

I'm sure that the older engineers of, let's say the high-end universities wouldn't refer to themselves as immigrants at all. They would likely say they invented the world in which the immigrants and natives now 'live'.

Some of the first-generation Silicon Valley tech engineers have even stated they invented some of these spaces and therefore how can they be an immigrant to their own designed world? And as a cheeky reflection here are they saying they have what is called a god complex?

Jest as I may, the technology you are now integrating into your life was indeed invented to enable us to live in a *new world*, one that has been proposed in many ways from the utopian, dystopian, and inaccurate, from sci-fi to sci-fact and beyond. We have many books on the subject, for example, *Brave new World* (Huxley, 1932/1994), *Neuromancer* (Gibson, 1984), all the ones by Phillip Dick for example (e.g. Dick, 1972), not to mention the films such as the Terminator, iRobot and more…

THE HERE AND NOW!

But this is too far in the future for this book and so I will name the technology I am addressing here in these chapters: handheld devices such as smartphones, tablets, gaming consoles, including the static race (fall guys), first-person shooters, Lego Star Wars, boxing, sport games, or games that simulate illegal activities such as driving into a building or over a person, or the shooting of aliens in the sky such as space invaders? What kind of violence? How is it represented, for example, little blood versus lots of it? A cartoon format or realistic? What about the games like whack-a-mole that you can buy in shops? Is this a violent form of game that has been replicated in the video game world? Violent, 'fun' or both?

What do we *mean* by these terms in the literature? I can say that many of the studies use many of these terms without defining accurately what they mean and this is the issue with an approach to research (epistemology) and how we speak to the subjective nature of these issues (phenomenology) and it is complicated as you can see.

Have you ever asked someone what they mean by gardening? Do they all reply with the same actions, or process, and do they name the same plants, vegetation, or environment? And do you have to have a house with a garden to engage in this behaviour? What about people who have veggie plots or allotments? How would you measure this term unless you specified it meant the 'act of gardening by the planting of daffodil bulbs only'. You would have a small sample of gardeners, and it would be very specific to daffodils and so assumptions about carrot growers or tree surgery would be vastly different behaviours and may not even be described as gardening!

You can see there are so many questions when we look at these words and phrases. They are not objective and so when it comes to measuring them, it is difficult to do so unless we describe exactly and specifically what we mean by them and this brings the object of the study into such a small and unique area that we could not generalise to the population (of humans, gender, age group etc.) and yet this is often exactly what is being done in this domain of research.

For example, compare the following approaches to a study remit; 'drugs cause violence' versus 'smoking x number of a specific brand of cigarettes per day, from the start to less than a cm before the stub, in males aged 70–75 is correlated with higher frequencies of chest infections in that population'. It would be 'bad science' to then say 'all smokers… x, y, z'. So how can we look at technology through this lens of daffodils versus carrots and trees? You might now see the complications.

'USE' OF GAMING AND SOCIAL MEDIA

How do these terms interact with the process of 'using', 'consuming', or 'interacting with' the behaviours and language relating to technology and the environments discussed above? And who do the studies point towards when we look at the populations under investigation? Quite often it's the cohort of young people, adolescents, tweens, teens, and more.

THE POPULATION LANGUAGE; OH MY!

Then we have:

- 'Young people'
- 'Adolescents'
- 'Children'
- 'Young adults'

What ages are these? And who decides what a child or young person is and how? When you think in terms of brain development, we know (who is we?) that some people do not fully 'mature' (again what does this mean?) until they are about 25–28 years of age. So, does this mean anyone under 25 and older than 12 is an adolescent or young person or are they still a child if they are under the age of 18? When does one become another or separate from?

DEVELOPMENT AND CHRONOLOGY

In addition to this, we can also add in another complexity about children and their trajectory through their lifetime. When, in my line of work I see many under 25 with developmental trauma or learning difficulties and educational needs which can and do change how that person relates to the world, I can understand their behavioural and emotional interactions and why they do not fit the 'normal' language so often afforded to many children.

An example of this is a person who may be chronologically 17 years of age, have had foetal alcohol impacts that have been present since birth, may behave in a developmentally delayed manner (compared to the curve of distribution of other 17-year-olds), and their understanding of the world and ability to think (cognition) and regulate their emotions may mirror that of an 11-year-old. How do we factor these children into the research when we make broad blanket statements about gaming and social media use, interactions and more? Because how a child here engages with others online may be vastly different from a child with learning difficulties based on language comprehension.

And what about differences in culture, race, or economic status where social media isn't even a thing yet due to lack of internet access? How do we compare the natives of 27 years' worth of use to the new visitors to the space who may also be chronologically the same age? The whole world is not online yet and given that much of the research has been taking place in the US, UK, India, Africa, or China, what about the other countries and people?

TECHNOLOGY AND HOW WE COPE

Often researchers are comparing the child, with social media actions, with an outcome behaviour or diagnosis such as self-harm, depression, suicide, addiction, or problematic behaviours, and again I ask what these terms mean, how are they measured accurately, given depression in one child may look significantly different from another?

How are these outcomes studied when we look at tiles such as these?

> Increase in depression, self-harm and suicide among US adolescents after 2012 and links to technology use. Possible mechanisms.
>
> (Twenge, 2020)

Or

> Relationship of socials and behavioural characteristics to suicidality in community adolescents with self-harm. Considering contagion and connection on social media.
>
> (Seong et al., 2021)

Or

> suicide closeting and contagion. The role of the media
>
> (Benson et al., 2021)

What do these studies actually study, how is it measured, what does it mean, and for whom?

I am exhausted after writing this. I suspect you are now more confused than having clarity and in the next few chapters I hope to explain these studies and how they impact your life. However:

> ***If you only read this page, or this summary chapter; this book is aiming to help you understand:***
>
> **It is *complicated***
>
> **It is *multifaceted***
>
> **It is human-ing *in a* world of technology *and* we don't *have* the *answers yet.* And it's *changing* once *again* with the introduction of *large language* models *and Artificial* Intelligence, so even if we did understand human-ing in *a* world of technology, it's *about* to change in *ways* we *are* not *prepared for,* so *get ready* to pivot.**

You need to make your own choices about your use of this technology as it fits you, your family, your situation, and your children at this time of your or their lives.

> **A problem is only *a* problem, if it is *a* problem.**

So you are saying all technology, gaming, and social media are okay then Cath? There are no ill effects, and we should not be worried, concerned, or take any action for ourselves or our children to manage our mental health and well-being in a world of technology?

I am far from saying this here in this chapter, or at all. However, I am saying that when we look at the discipline of technology research, and what is being talked about in large spaces such as e-safe-ness (which includes e-safety, trust and safety, online harm, and such titles), academia, large corporate, voluntary, and charity organisations dedicated to professing their expertise in this subject (which includes the face of these organisations suggesting they are *the one* with the answers), mainstream media, subject matter expert articles online and in training establishments that everyone has their vested interest in the lore, the outcomes, discussions, selling of 'wares', and sometimes the seeking of celebrity status.

What really matters is how this technology affects most of us, in the most common ways; for example it is not thinking like a rocket scientist that helps us understand that poverty has an impact on life quality (broad statement here I know!), and so technology must have an impact on us, in some way. Social media and gaming for some people are not the best ways to spend their time and for others it turns out to be a lifesaving space.

This is human-ing 101 and we all have a stake in how we interact with this emerging techne, how it changes us for both the better and the not so better, and what we can learn from this. The research is there to aid in our understanding, not to beat us with suggesting we are broken humans, when we the humans created the spaces in which we spend our time.

And maybe this is all moot anyway when AI really gets going…

And so this is the set and setting of this book from this point on.

I really wish I had in my hands the book *Unlocked* by Pete Etchells (2024) printed after this manuscript was completed. It's a fuller and deeper dive into some of the science and so this sentence was added in 2024 to show you the way to another great book. You'll find the details in the suggestions for further reading section. Grab that too for a balanced read. Thanks Pete for writing it!

2

WHY DO WE HAVE THE TECHNOLOGY HABITS WE DO?

HOW WE ARE PLAYED

If I told you that you were a lab rat or a pigeon, how would you feel about that? If it told you this was true in some way, would you stop reading here or would you like to know how you became a lab rat and find a way to 'stop it'?

What about if I explained that you are the equivalent of a primate with a brain region that can think, plan, and execute those plans and it is this element of your human-ness that has been carefully followed, manipulated, and curated into the person who has #fomo, addiction and all the other labels assigned to someone who uses gaming and social media and you were not consulted in the process about how you were part of an experiment? (Centre for Humane Technology, n.d.).

DO YOU FEEL THAT THIS IS UNFAIR?

Here you find out that you have been manipulated by a system, discipline, and set of people, services, and big data that are now 'measuring' your actions, reactions, and behaviours. Possibly rubbing their hands in glee at the money you might be making for them and of course imagining how they will spend this on their next vacation,

DOI: 10.4324/9781032617251-3

yacht or supercar at your expense. Are you angry, dismayed, in disbelief, shocked, or laughing at the ridiculousness of this proposal? Do you feel like you just read the script for a comedy film that is beyond the pale in the legalities of such a thing?

This sounds preposterous, right? Sadly, you are reading this book for a reason, and you may well know exactly what I'm talking about because you have been inundated with personalised ads, emails, and social media feed recommendations (for you!) for a long time. It is indeed the world of technology and the 'giants' who create the spaces we pay heavily to play in (not necessarily with money) and how it has been created to promise you *the fire you badly desire*. Most of us have sold our souls, signed into these spaces for pathological reasons (more on this later) and or we have been conned!

Or have we?

LAB RAT I AM NOT!

You see if you read *some* research work, news, and literature out there you will be convinced that the above words are true. Completely and utterly. If you then cross the road to where *some other* researchers and journalists are you'll find their approach is that this is nonsense and all doom and gloom narratives and that there is no robust evidence for such claims.

If you read books or have ever attended cybersecurity training you'll hear that '*you are the product*' of the technology companies output and you are effectively 'stupid'. You have been played, conned, tricked, manipulated and you *can't see it*. This is how *you*, the '*end user*' are often talked about in some books, and training events. How are you feeling about this?

Now don't get me wrong, the humans that technology staff must interact with from third-line support (call centres) to face-to-face repairs etc. have been called (in the past) *the* problem. There is an old acronym that was often used in the world of IT many moons ago, where the 'in joke' was PEBCAK (problem exists between chair and keyboard; https://en.wiktionary.org/wiki/PEBCAK) highlighting that it was always the '*end user's*' fault that something wasn't working or had broken because computers only compute and of course GIGO (garbage in = garbage out). Computers can only follow instructions that humans give them (for now), and so human beings must be the problem. I mean have you turned it off and back on again?

TURN IT ON AND KEEP *IT* ON

The big tech mantra perhaps? But here is the instruction manual to making cash flow easy: in the case of the spaces of social media and gaming, you are not the problem but *the solution*. If only we can just keep them (meaning you...) '*using*' these spaces, then attentional time = bank (lots of money)! And if you want to manipulate, first you must understand human behaviour and so consult psychology, sociology, and in some cases biology.

This is how big tech, gaming, and social media spaces keep you on their platform, it's how they monetise you. I will now explain some of this to you so you can understand how the large tech companies have developed their platforms and apps to enable you to spend your time there unwittingly, unknowingly, and understandably because you want to. And it is always *both!*

THE LANDSCAPE OF MARKETING, HUMAN BEHAVIOUR, AND ECONOMICS

This evolving myriad of professions is becoming more specialised and targeted with new titles for employment and research, and more disciplines have been opening up such as those called or looking at: behavioural economics (Corr & Plagnol, 2018), neuro-marketing (Morin & Renvoise, 2018), and the attention economy (Nelson-Field, 2020). In each one of these areas broad consultations take place about which humans and how they behave, what can be utilised, specifically focused on, and exploited to 'get your business'. So, let's back track a moment to the area of marketing per se and your local supermarket and TV channels to get an overview of this.

EXCITEMENT = FOMO!

If you have children or have ever watched channels that have children's programmes on you'll know how 'spritely', exciting, and joyful the children toy adverts are. Mostly resulting in that consistent 'pester power' of 'can I have one, can I have one can I have one... pleeeassse!!!' You may have even seen adverts for all the products that you 'need' in your house or stomach (think fast food here too) and each advert is designed to be remembered in some way directly or in your subconscious. Each advert is created by a team of specialists who are looking to get their product into your memory, by association, in some way, so that the next time you are heading towards the local supermarket, and you see their product you make an (often) unconscious choice to buy it (Heath, 2012). It might be because it had the best (or most annoying) tune, and packaging, or was something you didn't know you needed until the words and emphasis in the advert told you so. In supermarkets, you are looking at items placed at eye height, prominently for you to acknowledge, with offers that are just too good to be true, or just under the magic £1, and lo and behold it's in your trolley or basket and on its way to the cashier as it's not as expensive as the £1 item right?

NEEDED VERSUS WANTED

We often do need these products, for example, laundry cleaner, tinned foods, fresh fruit, frozen items, and more so this whole process is more about the 'best' promotion that captures our attention enough for us to have a super quick think (both in and out of our awareness) about cost, suitability, desirability, the amount we already have at home and therefore our own estimation on 'stock levels', and sometimes the advert and how we 'felt' after watching it. And this *want versus need* is a common narrative in the addiction literature (Grigutsch et al., 2019). Desirability is a potent emotion calling us.

FEELINGS, THOUGHTS, AND BEHAVIOURS

This last aspect, *feelings*, is probably the most powerful driver of being a human when it comes to the process that can be toyed with the most by others (this is quite the big revelation to therapy clients) as feelings often underpin the thinking about a product and what it will or can do for us.

The processes of behaviour generally follow feelings and thoughts and the best way to illustrate this is to think about some adverts such as the yearly Christmas tear-jerker, or the ones about children starving, in war-torn countries, or the ones about animal cruelty and dog shelters for example. Hopefully for this thought experiment you have seen one and recognised how they are emotive, and the designers thought about the things that make us angry, hostile, separated, sad, connected, inspired, or joyful and what we do following these adverts can be motivating enough for us to donate to the cause, remember the product, or talk about it with others (this one now also means sharing it on social media).

NEGATIVE AND EMOTIVE, SUBTLE, OR DIRECT

In the example of the adverts, negative emotions (sometimes disguised as positive, happy, and 'good') are used most frequently because they feel unpleasant and tap into a specific pattern of behaviour that we engage in when our nervous systems are pinged in some way. Now what does that mean? You may have heard of the fight-and-flight mechanism that our bodies and brains use to keep us safe and to help protect us as a species (Le Doux, 2015). Whether you have or haven't I wanted you to be aware of this stress mechanism that has been labelled as the 'limbic hijack' which doesn't entirely cover our biology and behaviour in full but is quite the catchy way to refer to humans' behaviour (by documentaries such as the Social Dilemma, https://www.youtube.com/watch?v=yGi2YKZZNFg) as it suggests that you have no power over it (explained below).

EVOLUTION AND BIOLOGY ADAPTATIONS

Let us start with some simple lessons and explanations regarding the chapter title about how we are subject to the ever-changing whims of our biology, feelings, and behaviours and how these systems are exploited in us (all) for the spaces of social media and gaming. We are at the mercy of these process at such a high frequency that we would be mechanical if that was not the case. Here I posit that because it is suggested the numbers of human pathologies and labels of attentional deficit and social skills are increasing, this could almost be an evolutionary counterattack to what is happening to us right now (in the attempt to manipulate our attention and social needs). We fight attentional grabbing with attentional reductions and lack of empathy to combat the pull on our compassion and connection

(Much more research is needed on this idea before I go off on a tangent regarding this!)

BIOLOGY 101, BEHAVIOUR 101, AND HUMAN-ING 101

Fact: we are born helpless and in need of other human beings to survive. Part of this process is learning how to be kept alive *by others* until we can take care of ourselves (Bowlby, 1997). The infant communicates this through innate survival mechanisms such as the ability to cry about something that *it is feeling*. This is usually hunger, temperature, fear or anxiety about a bodily sensation such as wind or hiccups, and the desire to be close to another human for safety. Our survival needs are the priority, and we also need another human to meet those needs, whether they be feeding us, changing our nappy (or diaper) or holding us whilst we fall asleep. Feelings are big and important, and we learn to adapt these feelings to the family in which we are raised. The long and the short of this is that we pay attention to our feelings first and foremost in many situations and we often follow these feelings, which is where the exploitation takes place in relationships, friendships, and employment.

Our nervous systems play a large part in this by providing us with the feeling of safety both inside our bodies (called neuroception (Porges, 2011)) and between people, places, and things. We refer to these safety mechanisms as intrapersonal (in ourselves) and interpersonal (between us) and this process is what guides our flight, fight, freeze, and flop set of behaviours when we do not feel safe. This process is guided by the body and brain (initially taking place 'lower' than the limbic system quoted earlier in the chapter).

This follows a familiar pattern, based on our histories and the *perceived level of threat the nervous system and lower areas of the brain assign to the sensory information.* For a more detailed explanation of this see my previous books, my YouTube video of the polyvagal motorway of wellness (https://www.youtube.com/watch?v=QGBv1KrJ5P), and the work of Stephen Porges (2021) and colleagues in the interpersonal neurobiological discipline (Siegel, 2012) (for understanding stress and trauma).

TAPPING INTO STRESS MECHANISMS: DEFAULT SETTINGS

This nervous system activation takes place out of our awareness most of the time, and we only tend to notice it when perhaps we feel anxious, notice our heartbeat racing, or the sensations of sweaty palms for example. However, exactly what sensory information our brain attends to, to make sense of a perceived threat, is too large to describe here so a summary is provided: the brain 'listens to and decodes' bodily signals, or thoughts arising and creates a habituated stress response to 'save time' next time.

The limbic hijack that was mentioned earlier is the latter stage of this process and often results in a physical reaction to the said event.

This behaviour can be a physical urge to flee, to fight, or stay very still, and in some cases this response is fragmentation of the moment. This is a last resort so to speak and takes place by us disconnecting (dissociating) from the experience. This hierarchy of habituated and well-practised behaviours is, if you like, 'chosen' as the one with the highest chance of survival and can often become the default setting for stress responses. It is out of our noticing because that would take too much brain time to process and so we have those 'knee-jerk' reactions without fully understanding why in some cases.

WHY IS THIS IMPORTANT HERE FOR THE MECHANICS OF SOCIAL MEDIA AND GAMING?

If the above suggests reductionistic biology and we don't get to choose how we respond to a stimulus, then it doesn't sound much like free will does it? And perhaps in the truest sense of the word it is not a choice we make with full consent. This system and process are so easy to play with by big tech because stress (or 'fear) is the one reaction we rely on the most to survive. Hence the manipulation of these 'circuits' keeps us on the platform through negative news, polarised ideology, and what we see and read that evokes the stress response.

Prompts, pings and pushes, nudges, and rewards

In marketing, some problems are proposed to us so that we engage with the product (or service) and tap into the same circuity discussed above.

One example is that we ought to desire something because of X, Y, or Z. For example, certain aftershaves, colognes, and perfumes make you more desirable; and so, by not having them, you are essentially unhygienic, smelly, and unwanted. Of course, this is what you want to avoid whilst achieving something that makes you feel 'good'.

Another is sold to us as the 'you are missing out, people will think less of you if you don't have it, this is important and you're making a mistake if you don't buy this'. For example, *needing* the latest iPhone to look like you have money and status or are not left behind.

The advertising is aimed at you not having *an item, to increase your likelihood of wanting to have that item*, to relieve that feeling, the deficit of *not-having-ness* (Shotton, 2023). It's aimed at your 'weaknesses' of feeling a failure, incomplete, useless, to prevent humiliation or shame, to let you imagine the future where you have conquered this.

Many adverts show you that future and you may be mistaken to think the advert is showing you what the product can and will do for you, but it's based on highlighting the fact *you don't have* this (influence, popularity, adoration etc.).

And if you do, maybe this is the next iteration such as the whitest white white white laundry cleaning product since the whitest white one of yesterday!! Keep up, the Joneses already have it, why don't you?

These sometimes subtle and hidden *prompts* are aimed at feelings that were built in childhood about avoiding rejection, shame, and humiliation. (If you listen to children, they explain quite clearly why they *want* something.) Associative memory systems (Fonagy, 2001) look for familiarities in the world, or whether something is worth paying attention to and these adverts remind you of a time when…

The techniques used in advertising speak to this area of memory subtly and overtly. Unless you find you are consciously singing the latest tune to an advert because it happens to be by a band you like for example, then it's likely it bypassed your awareness and became another one of those laughable, annoying, or 'weird' earworm adverts that you find popping into your head when you see a product in the supermarket aisles, or even singing it before the advert has played it fully.

Subtle works but so does the type of advert that tells you directly that you *need* this, you *must have it*, get it *quick*, you don't have time to wait, and the sales end soon and if you buy now you can have a discount, a freebie, or some other '*that's not all*' technique (Brennan & Bahn, 1991) uses in sales.

These 'tricks' are taken right out to the books on psychology and human behaviour. Attention economics (Nelson-Field, 2020) as it is called nowadays utilises work from a prominent name in psychology (and others) of why we do what we do. William James (2017) proposed two things of importance here:

1. *Bodies react physiologically, and behaviour follows this*: i.e. we hear something unknown and then we run. We decided afterwards that we must have felt fear or been scared. We put what Deb Dana (2018) calls 'story follows state' to understand the event. Our story to ourselves explains what occurred in the state we were (or are) in. In the case of adverts, the story follows the feelings created by the advert material and content.
2. *Attention is the deliberate focusing on an item at the discretion of ignoring everything else*: i.e. we learn to listen to a specific singular voice like our mother when noise elsewhere may be loud (Music, 2017) (babies learn to do this very quickly). And so adverts can be loud (colour, noise, or speed for example), jingly or quiet to pique interest and engage our listening systems and this attentional focus now means we pay direct and specific 'attending' focus to the content at the expense of something else. Have you ever tried to talk to a child who is watching a mesmerising advert?

And so, if the advertisers can get you to feel something physiologically, such as an aroused nervous system by shouting at the start of the advert (think the Cillit-Bang adverts for example, https://www.youtube.com/watch?v=lrMD_z_FnNk) then they can drive your focus to the immediate message at hand, which you now pay attention to whether you want to or not, and it only needs to be for a short time. And by the time you decide the advert is naff, it's already landed in those levels in your brain you cannot communicate with directly.

B J FOGG AND BEHAVIOURAL ECONOMICS

Furthermore, there is even a university degree aimed at educating you in behavioural economics as a discipline, primarily based on the theories of behavioural psychology mostly famous for dogs, pigeons, and rats. And many of the big tech moguls started studying courses like this to increase engagement on their platforms, even citing this in documentaries such as The Social Dilemma (https://www.youtube.com/watch?v=yGi2YKZZNFg).

This approach to science (behaviourism at the basic core (Woolard, 2010)) is not interested in your thoughts or feelings as they affect you personally (as in any pain they may cause) because true behaviourists are not interested in studying these elements, but they would be interested in how they affect you in so far as being able to play with, manipulate, and maximise these feelings to their advantage.

Those behavioural actions can be manipulated by certain elements in the content we engage with online or in games and form, let's call it a chain reaction process which now creates a feeling of wanting to stay on the platform or game, or return to it if we are away from it. This chain reaction forms over time with incremental additions to your emotions depending upon what you engage with, or the level you achieve, or it can be instantaneous if the trigger or stimulus is effective enough for you. This is how we teach old dogs new tricks as the saying goes.

For example, you may have heard the stories of dogs who salivated at the sound of a bell, pigeons who could discriminate colours and shapes, rats who could learn a maze or the ones who drank themselves stupid on opioid-based water, or dolphins trained to find missiles and how these all represent you, the human being (Bennett-Levy et al., 2004). And that is how we get played. And yes we can indeed be pinged, promoted, and pushed to these behaviours by big tech and they know it.

[At the time of writing Meta and its subsidiary/sister organisations were being sued for creating addictive processes like this for teens on their platforms because they have less self-awareness of these manipulations than the adults do (if any adults know this has happened to them).]

WHAT *NEEDS OR WANTS* IN YOU ARE BEING EXPLOITED THROUGH GAMING AND SOCIAL MEDIA?

Gaming

Play, cortisol, challenge, excitement, mastery, and fun. Novelty, neurotransmitters, and notability. And I could end there in terms of what games exploit. I am sure none of these surprised you.

Because we are talking about an innate function of (most of) the human beings that exist. We are born to play (Fortune, 2022) and through this activity we learn many new skills that we can transition across into other situations. In psychology the term used for this transfer of knowledge and skills is generalisation, i.e. we take a skill and learn to adapt that skill in some way to a new and novel situation, or we recognise a process as being similar to another situation (hence why most of the user experiences on tablets and smartphones follow the same kinds of patterns).

In gaming, we are playing, rehearsing, and practising in the same way that babies learn to develop language and motor movements. We are using these skills to form new neuronal pathways of thought, solve problems, and master the art of motor skills and dexterity. We are using cognition (thinking) and assessing the suitability of an action or behaviour to the task in hand (literally, if you are holding a controller, using a keyboard, or handheld device).

We are excited (neuronally, psychologically, and physically) by a challenge and if it just happens to be a teeny weeny bit more complex than we are used to, or feels like we have to actively think a little about what actions to take next, then we are pulled sweetly along by neurotransmitters into a state called 'flow' (Csikszentmihalyi, 1992/2002) where our challenge and skills meet, where this flow state emerges and is intoxicating.

However, if the task is too difficult then we fall foul of frustration. Some people do not want to try and overcome frustration and so go and find something else to do, but others may find themselves fixated on solving the problem until they get the insight of the solution (what is called the aha moment) which purges forward into the cycle of flow and can result in a more intense experience of flow.

So how do games exploit you, your needs, or these processes? Or could this be a variant form of keeping your attention and time such that the designers want the game to be fun, engaging and to create that feeling of 'let's do it again!' because who wants to play a dull game huh? The very fact that the computer game exists means it must be a sweet spot of interest and excitement and that could be in the form of the story, graphics, or both. It must have appeal and often games are designed from things that are already appealing to us in the form of movies, comics, and books. Players play because they identify in some way with the idea of the game and so before you even click to start you have an investment in the playing of the game (Lieberman & Long, 2019). This differs from social media in the way in which we often have an interest in the game for our own motivations. Just look to the people who love to complete a crossword in the newspapers or magazines, they can tell you whereabouts in the paper or magazine the crossword is because they find themselves returning to complete this like someone does with Tetris, God of War, or Lego Star Wars to name a few. There is a motivational process that occurs before the engagement with the puzzle, and this can also be why people choose certain genres of games too. Certain authors and books sell for this reasontoo, along with TV shows that are 'binged' on.

Isn't this interest and excitement, investment in the character and story what TV shows are all about with their cliffhangers? Even board and card games can induce this feeling of enjoyment and you want to replay, maybe you can go for the best out of three, or in the case of Bill & Ted versus The Grim Reaper (https://www.youtube.com/watch?v=cPc-MeuUU10): the best of five, seven, and 11.

Enjoyment or the want to win?

Or is it as simple as wanting to win the game? Do designers really want to exploit the negatives of human behaviour, or do most of them want to create a space of fun, enjoyment, community, laughter, challenge, creativity, and curiosity? Is the gaming world a menace to society or are we really driven to *play* in the truest sense and gaming meets that need? What if games provide a space for people to connect, to compete safely (rather than sublimate their anger in the real world for example), to combat other feelings that exist in their lives such as loneliness, anxiety, depression, and games provide a respite from this in the same way music, activities, and other experiences can and do?

Is gaming exploiting us and our attention? Or do we freely give this only to become enraptured in the process and story and lose our sense of self, time, and effort in a rich experience? If you look to the research on flow states, you often find it mentioned as a great way to counteract trauma, depression, and negative thoughts (aside from the frustration ones related to the game). Immersive stories, accompanied by our love of music is in our DNA so to speak and the gaming industry can give us something of this. Exploited… or provided?

However, when in the flow state, that lack of sense of self and time can lead to not paying attention to full bladder signs, posture, or the connection to the corporeal world and this seems to be the biggest negative that impacts on a person's life, when they are playing for excessive 'sitting' hours and not moving their body (a little like writing a book can be!) and so health impacts are important here, and the impact that can occur by not 'taking part' in the real world and opting for the one provided by games. Where children don't go to school or adults don't go to work.

How do we rectify the idea that gaming is both positive and negative? How do you use the information here to understand that gaming does exploit mechanisms of innate drives such as play, and the want to be with others like you (albeit often as a 'by-product' rather than an outright demonised exploitative process)? How do you become aware of this to manage your gaming habits?

Gaming can meet lots of primary needs and therefore this will require some considered thinking about the time you spend gaming, how you want to integrate this into your life and schedules, and how this 'gaming time' can be used for and against children as a punitive 'reward and or punishment'. Knowing what gaming is and why we play can help us create some boundaries for ourselves or our children, and learning about setting and keeping those boundaries is discussed throughout this book.

XP, Trophies, and Skins: Olympic medals!

To end the section here on gaming I want to speak to notoriety when it comes to gaming and this is often an area exploited by other people in the real world, as well as by the gaming companies through the visibility of experience points (XP), prestige status and trophies, skins, and other visible attributes that show how 'good' a player is. This is perhaps the one area that overlaps with childhood development and their needs the most, and which can be seen in the feelings of importance, being noticed, revered, and at times adored. This is why people spend lots of time in and on games because you don't get to the top spot by *playing occasionally*.

This is about people who want to be seen to be the best at something and is akin to the Olympic *Games*. Notice the language of 'games' here denoting that even real-world sport creates the same behaviours, and I suspect that *Olympic Addiction Disorder* could be a thing if I pushed it hard enough in the media with the same attributes of gaming disorder and addiction narratives, and created a clinic for the athletes, sportspeople, and committees involved in this. I would charge 'bank' for this and be very rich and famous. I could write books on the matter too.

Social media

Needs, notifications, and near misses

I am going to cheat a little for this section to save on time, word count, and direct you to my TEDx talk (Knibbs, 2022a) (for the counts and clout of course!) and to summarise the books that have already been written by many around attachment theory and how I use these in my earlier books to explain our behaviour online. This section could go on for hours, so I will keep it as short as possible.

This is about human communication, connections, and the behaviours that we engage in to meet those *needs* and these were exploited by big tech and we didn't see it till it was 'too late' in the game.

The summary of attachment theory (Bowlby, 1997) is we are born ready to socialise and in doing so we have a primary need to get others to take care of us to prevent us from being rejected, abandoned, and causing us to die. That's it in a nutshell as everything comes back to this really. And that avoidance of rejection and abandonment underpins most of what you do, daily. Especially on social media. *Thank you for coming to my TEDx talk.*

'Attention retention' = big bucks and bank

Big tech uses attention economics (Nelson-Field, 2020), however if you understand this process of attachment, you can see that *attention needing* is this process in its most basic and simple form. This is discussed in more detail in the help chapters (5 and 6) to give you insight into why you do what you do on these platforms. Those notifications (icons or sounds) are alarms that tap into these needs. This has been called 'the race to the bottom of the limbic system' by Tristan Harris (2016) when he speaks out on this matter, but he tends to frame it as 'attentional' processes of what is called (in cognitive psychology) 'attending to' a particular 'thing' which is actually a mix of cortical function as well as limbic system processes, but it sounds catchy doesn't it, 'race to the bottom of your brain?' Our bio-survival circuitry is deeply rooted, deeply needed, and deeply exploited. The book *Children, Technology and Healthy Development* (Knibbs, 2022b) explains in detail the neuroscience and attachment of these processes and how social media taps into these to keep us using their platforms.

Polyvagal processes

Our nervous systems are the communication pathways of these needs moving from the brainstem to the body and back again. I explain these pathways as being like a car on the motorway where middle-lane driving gives us choices about how we respond to the world, which includes the things we interact with or see on social media. We can either mobilise our attention and energy to engage with these posts and people or we can mobilise away from, and this looks like we move into the other lanes and back again with our free will and choice. However, like cars on the motorway, we can be pushed from the middle lane into the outer lanes by a near miss (or push) of other vehicles (our underlying history patterns) and it is understanding why we are drawn to react in this way that can help us understand our behaviours online (The Polyvagal motorway of wellness, n.d.).

Jiminy Cricket

Science has shown over many years of studies and theories that we are 'in relation' to other people (interpersonal) even when we are not with them physically, for example, think here about that nagging voice you hear when you're about to make a 'not so great' decision, it's the Jiminy Cricket voice in your head (https://disney.fandom.com/wiki/Jiminy_Cricket). We are in relation to and with the person when we see something they have texted (or written online) and you probably read it in their voice if you know them, or your own if you don't (the same applies to video content, but slightly differently). This is called a parasocial relationship (Kowett, 2021) and we are often caught up in the same mechanism of attachment here, albeit at a slower pace in comparison to a conversation taking place between you (even if you can type fast!).

The exploitative process that the big tech engages us with is the feeling of being connected to others, or wanting to be, and that feeling of not being connected, the one called fear of missing out. These mechanisms can be pushed and pulled with those notification pings, and it is the social 'validation or verification' (Hillman et al., 2023) feeling that we seek that keeps us coming back. This validation is the one that we know so well when we are those babies and the adults around us delight in our presence, or not and this early experience can set the stage for how and why we seek others in this space and why we might engage in certain behaviours with them (arguing, liking, commenting, sharing and so on). It's all about seeking deep connection, and often not finding that in the social media space.

How do I change this? Read on...

3

GAMING AND MENTAL HEALTH. WHAT'S THE SCIENCE OR RESEARCH HERE?

NOT ALL GAMES ARE EQUAL

I'm going to describe the kinds of computer (video) games that we would be looking at when we think about this kind of research. What do we mean by gaming, gamer, computer games, video games, mobile games, immersive technology games, tabletop games, hybrid games, puzzle games, and more?

TYPOLOGY[1] AND DEFINITIONS: PHYSICAL ENVIRONMENTS/PLATFORMS

- *Computer games* are created to allow the person to play a game on a (home) computer. This took off in the late 1980s when arcade games were copied into a format that could be played at home using a keyboard and joystick. The graphics at the start of computer gaming were simple (8-bit) as the processors in the computers were quite small. Nowadays they are almost as good as a cinema production using high-end graphics cards in the computer, with super quick processors.

DOI: 10.4324/9781032617251-4

- *Video games* are as above and were created as a term to describe games (as early as the 1970s such as Pong) that could be played on a television screen via a console or computer.
- *Mobile game* describes a game which might be described as a video game or computer game that can take place via a mobile internet-ready device such as a smartphone or tablet.
- *Immersive technology games* are ones played within an immersive environment such as VR (virtual reality), XR (extended reality), AR (augmented reality), and MX (mixed reality). These are not all based inside headsets but can overlap with the shared/blended category below.
- *Arcade: simulation games* might be found at fairgrounds and arcades and might be akin to a life-size plastic replica of a motorbike, for example where the game involves racing a motorbike. Or perhaps a plastic replica rifle where a shooting game takes place. These are likely to be found in arcade settings more than within a home (depending on the amount of money one has or not).
- *Shared/blended interactive games* such as the Wii or Kinect which involve both a computer or video game system utilising a camera to blend what the person is doing in a physical space with what's occurring in the game. Both the Wii and Kinect are in retirement in most homes I believe. Added to this are games that blend board games with a short film, or set of choices used via a remote control to give players direction for the board game and these are not as popular as the ones above.

(Omitted from this list: I did not mention educational games that might be utilised within education or learning environments such as schools, colleges, or universities. When we think about this area of 'gaming' research they may not be included in the same way that home gaming is. The reason for this is not exactly clear.)

Typology and definitions: genres of games

When we think of gaming as being similar in terminology to 'music' we are looking at many genres. Given the list above which includes a myriad of gaming environments, we would also need to consider the typology of the game, or genre that a person might be playing, or is under the study remit. Often when we see gaming studies in mainstream media, they refer to the 'violent video game' category. Even this labelling brings about some issues of meaning and type.

To set the scene; the following list applies to the typology of gaming. This new lingo may seem like a list of acronyms as often they are shortened to this.

Heading back to the very first type of computer game that appeared in people's homes in the 1970s. I don't know how to correctly classify 'Pong' as this was a game that resembled tennis but played with two straight lines as the bats or rockets and a ball where the pixels made it almost spherical. I thought it quite apt to place it here but outside of the list below.

Genre[2] (or type of game)

- *Platform games* (2D) are early arcade games such as Spaceship (Asteroid), Alien (Space Invaders), Street Fighter, Pac-Man, Kong, Jet Set Willy, and the early Mario games and ones in which the graphics are 2D and movements of the figure occur using arrows or a joystick enabling the user to play a fairly simplistic format.
- *Aircraft games* in the early days were clunky 2D moving to a 3D map-style game and now are a complex simulation-style with much more information in them. These would have required the use of movement keys on a keyboard or a joystick requiring the user to navigate the aircraft, and now have such complex systems for navigation that they resemble actual aircraft flight.
- *Role-playing or strategy-type games* in the early days of home computing was simple and utilised only text rather than images. Interacting with these games consisted of using limited choices or perhaps typing out simple instructions. These were early story-type games, for example, The Hobbit. These are much more complex nowadays and sometimes require the solving of puzzles, interacting with characters in the game, and even with other players (in online shared campaigns).

- *Action games* may well include a *fighting* style (Streetfighter) as named above, or those in which there is a *battle* to be won as part of the story, which can include alien, war (combat), film based storylines (Star Wars for example), driving and *competitive* aspects. The action category often denotes a fast-paced game with decision-making and a fast set of fingers or thumbs on the keyboard or controller.
- *Combat games* tend to blend into what is now called *first-person shooters* where combat missions take place, such as those the armed forces and military would engage in. These could also fall under the *strategy* category and so we start to see terminology overlapping and creating more confusion in the space of games than clarity.
- *Simulation games* early versions look similar to the aircraft or driving styles. Nowadays you are *replicating the real world* or creating something similar to the real world such as a family, city, theme park, or work environment.
- *Puzzle games* are similar to the *role-playing games* discussed a moment ago however these may also include mazes, puzzles such as images of locks with number combinations to solve, and perhaps even maps with clues hidden in plain sight. These also form part of the platform, role-playing, and strategy game genres as the gamer decodes what the clues mean to move through the game.
- *Card-type games* (or *board games*) such as solitaire which might be the most famous game that people recognise. There may have been variations on simple board games like backgammon or chess and it can be difficult to classify whether these would also be *simulation games*, *computer games*, *hybrid board games*, or *pub games*.
- *Shoot 'em up* games such as Doom, Halo, and Call of Duty, or Space Invaders. Doom, a computer game from the 1990s might well now be classified in a different genre and perhaps called a first-person shooter.

These may now be called action, strategy, battle, first-person shooter, simulation emulation or imagination! Who knows?

THE COMMON LANGUAGE OF GENRES (IN THE 21ST CENTURY)

There will be some repetition here.

- *FPS* (first-person shooter) is a game where you take the perspective of somebody with a weapon and as the game suggests you are involved in shooting that weapon (often this is a rifle or pistol). These games tend to be the most proactively researched because of the links that are suggested by politicians and mainstream media as having a link with people who engage in utilising these weapons in corporeal settings (often called shooters in the US). Sadly, these real-world events have taken place within school settings, churches, or open-air events. This specific genre is the one most often referred to as the violent video type, discussed in the news, by parents and teachers or mainstream media. When we think about the link between playing a game and a person's mental health during and after playing the game, speculation exists about what that may or may not lead to in terms of carrying out violence in the real world.
- *RPG* (role-playing games) may include optional games where a person can carry out a lone version of the story called a campaign by themselves. The lone player interacts with the computer throughout the game creating a story and journey with levels and spaces where puzzles may need to be resolved to progress. These games may also be played with one or lots of other players, from anywhere around the world in what is called massive multiplayer online role-playing games.
- *MMORPGs*. Furthermore, these role-playing games can include other types of games within them. For example, in the game The Witcher there is a card-playing game, called Gwent, that you play with a generated character. You can also engage in (usually predetermined) limited conversations with computer-generated figures called non-player characters (*NPCs*). This is about to change though, as at the time of writing I have seen AI-generated

characters (no longer being classified as an NPC) because they can take part in *an emerging conversation*. You will interact with the character in the same way you would interact with a real-life person (however the character must have some parameters with which to pass on the information needed for the game).

- *Strategy games* are a form of puzzle-solving, strategic manoeuvre, or detective-type games which also look like role-playing games. These can look like puzzle games with an interactive element, and some may include tactical decisions for a team you are in charge of (think of the board game risk). Or you are in a walk-through, varying levelled game where each environment requires a different strategy and set of skills. Moreover, strategy games can also be played in the genre of role-playing, or action or FPS games where entire battles take place online with other players (these are often called squads in colloquial terminology).
- *Mobile puzzle games* such as Sudoku or Tetris might be played on mobile phones for example, or many of the 2D colour-matching shape games (simple in design but may include increasing levels of complexity). Many of these games are often called boredom breakers or brain trainers. This is not a classification of games yet it is terminology that is used.
- *Simulation games* may include designs and approaches such as flying planes, driving trains, and now the re-enactment of the environment such as within the home and doing the cooking, washing down a driveway with a power jet, painting, gardening, and such activities. These games are incredibly realistic in immersive environments. Other types of simulation games include car racing and these can be in-game versions (for example in Roblox). My favourite titled simulation game is 'goat simulator'. Yes for real.
- *Augmented games* have been developed to allow us to use a device such as a handheld console like a Nintendo Switch or a mobile phone in the real world to interact with items that do not exist in the real world. One of the most popular augmented games of recent times is Pokémon Go which also overlaps into other categories and genres. In this game, you use the phone to map

and collect Pokémon in your corporeal world, even though at the physical locations there is no Pokémon to pick up and hold.

- *Sporting games* is quite a large category and might include games like FIFA (football) where you are controlling an entire football team and act as both manager and player(s). You may be a golfer, or perhaps you are taking part in bowling, or tennis. If you play these games on a console such as the Wii or Kinect, or in a VR headset, maybe taking part in an exercise class this may converge or overlap with other genres of gaming. Exercise, fitness, or gaming? I wonder if we would include treadmills at the gym or the Peloton where as you exercise the environment in which you exercise is created on the screen in front of you? If it is challenging and you can level up, create scores and compete is this classed as sport gaming?
- *Jump scare or horror games* got their name pretty much as described 'on the tin'. You might be playing a strategy-based game which is based on horror such as 'Resident Evil', or 'The Last of Us'. It could be an anticipation game such as 'Five Nights at Freddy's'. This is now available to play in VR and so might be found in that genre too.
- *Esports* is a mixture of the games described above, but includes a large platform of players and spectators, mostly in one space (such as an arena) and can be conceived as being like the Super Bowl the World Cup and the Olympics all in one.
- *Games with a specific goal for health and well-being (as well as fun)*commonly called exergames such as boxing on the Wii or VR (see sporting games)
- *Bio and neurofeedback* are usually played in a medical environment or therapeutic space but these are indeed games, which are utilised in practice to enable a person to change the way their mind and body works and is based on the concept of gaming. For example, I have used for over a decade in my clinical work games developed by companies such as Heart Math, Complete Coherence, Muse, and others. These are all based on biofeedback so that the player can learn to harness how they regulate their breathing and or stillness (mindfulness). These games are rooted in research and many others are coming onto the market as we speak.

CONTROLLERS

As games progressed from the basic forms, and technology provided us with consoles that contained more memory and processing speeds, the complexity of games increased to the point that they required a more complex set of controls. For example, a joystick alone would no longer suffice to move the characters, select items for the game, or change aspects of your clothing, armour, weapons, creative tools etc. The introduction of the handheld controller included selection buttons, sticks, and toggles and now through continued designing many parts of the controller fit within the hand and require all digits to partake. You may see gaming keyboards whereby certain keys are designed in an ergonomic design for the player as more than four keys are used in games nowadays.

Moreover, when we look at mobile, tablet-type games there can also be gravity-based settings such as tilt and roll which require the user to move the tablet or mobile device in those planes of movement. The intricacy of hand-eye coordination with a controller means that games are so much more complex nowadays. And so much faster in many cases.

GAMING ON A SCREEN, IN A HEADSET, OR IN BETWEEN WORLDS?

Blended, mixed, augmented, virtual realities commonly referred to as extended reality, can now take those games discussed here, level them up and create the illusion to both mind and body that you are very much in a different time and place. This paradigm of games is now going to include versions of touch, haptics, and sensory spaces that will again create more complexity for this research area. It's thrilling, exciting, and worrying all at the same time.

THERE! IT'S ALL AS CLEAR AS MUD NOW?

Clarity in research is the bee's knees so to speak. And I am sure that as you read through the above you can now see that all games are not equal and much like social media have lots of types (which means lots of reasons for wanting to play them).

When you see labels like gaming disorder (World Health Organization, 2022), gaming addiction (NHS Gaming Addiction, n.d.), and gaming dependency (Peng & Liu, 2010) then you can see that each of these might well be discussing differing forms of gaming, but sadly they refer to all types and it is not clear in any of the diagnostic manuals what 'kind' of gaming disorder this refers to.

Therefore, that leaves you as the reader of articles, literature, and listening to parenting conversations, trying to second guess what kind of gaming 'issue' for it to be an addiction disorder or dependence and to be perfectly honest how would you know? I hope you know that *newspaper crossword addiction* is a real thing. *Sudoku dependency* and *Word search disorder* too. I suspect the older folk who engage in these activities need to sign themselves into a rehabilitation clinic before it really is too late!

WHAT DOES THE LITERATURE SAY, WHAT *IS* THE RESEARCH IN THIS FIELD?

Even when we see headlines or research study titles like 'violent video games cause XYZ' this can be littered with confusing terminology, descriptions, and definitions. For example, the Kong platform game from the 1980s is violent if you consider the rolling barrels that squash the character. And, losing your life (meaning you must start again) is violent in concept. If you look at the type/genre of game called a first-person shooter this is suggesting violence. In this type of game, you could be attempting to shoot an alien or another person. Even with this, it depends on the graphic depiction as to whether you see the violence moment by moment and to what degree. For example, in Minecraft, with low-quality graphics, you can literally 'whack somebody/thing with a sword' and shoot them with a bow or a rifle and see no blood. Yet if you look at games like Call of Duty or other sniper-based games with high-end graphics you will see much more realistic 'endings'. How does this level of violence or graphic depiction have an impact? Or is it the frequency with which the game is played?

For a brilliant in-depth conversation around violent video games look to the work written by Chris Ferguson and Pat Markey, for example, their book *Mortal Combat* (Markey & Ferguson, 2017), and the work of Andrew Przybylski and Weinstein (2019), within the Oxford Internet Institute (and the numerous studies and research at the back of the book).

Expressed violence but not enacted

Violence can be an expression of power and does not always accompany anger (Gross, 1998). When working in a therapeutic setting I often use a sand tray (that is, actual sand in a tray), and I ask the children or adults I work with (many of whom have suffered traumas), to go and select some figures to place in the sand tray to tell a story. Quite often those moments of play within the sandtray are like a re-enactment of a battle, with dragons and knights, pirates, people with swords, Apex animals that kill and so on. Not once have I ever diagnosed a child or adult with *violent sandtray play disorder*.

When I look at the literature that surrounds sand play work (Bradway & McCoard, 1997; Marrodan & Moraga, 2024), depth psychotherapy, and play therapy, this idea of fantasy and violence makes up much of the expressive parts of the psyche. It can be a way a child gains mastery over a situation or re-tells a story of difficult things within their life (Oaklander, 1978). Therefore, the use of violent video games could also allow a child or adult to create an environment where destruction and death take place safely as no real person is harmed (unless the controller is thrown or lands on a person or animal).

If I look at the literature around violent video games, some suggest there is a causal link of violence in games producing violence in the real world (Anderson & Bushman, 2001), in the same way watching violent TV or film does (Anderson & Bushman, 2018). If I follow this line of thinking then perhaps I should rethink the way that children play in both the sand and with the games I use in therapy, because this would point to a link that 'violent play in therapy causes violent children'. I cannot find research supporting this claim and I don't think this sounds sensible at all. And some of these children play violent games more in therapy than they do gaming at home. It doesn't make sense to say it is only violent computer games that result in that outcome.

A TOOL WITH TWO OUTCOMES: IS THAT NOT THE MINDSET OF THE INDIVIDUAL?

Cigarettes are often called a multipurpose tool when you hear how they can both be a relaxant and a stimulant (Ashton et al., 1973). No other substance has this magic power. This contradictory statement is the same thinking that is applied to violent computer games when we say that violence creates violence, and yet in a therapeutic space metaphorical violence reduces violence. How can it be both? It sounds like the cigarette example where it is the user who decides what the outcome of the 'intervention' is. For example, 'It helps me relieve my stress and get it all out'.

ARCADE GAME ADDICTION

My question to end this thinking here is, where is the literature showing that arcade gaming produced violent humans, apart from the anecdotal evidence of people fighting to get on the machines (time in the location was limited by opening hours)? Is the VVG debate so prevalent because it transitioned into a home, on to a TV or computer that the violence in the human playing them was more visible? Or is it because of the violence surrounding the family feuds about *coming off the game* which I discuss at length in my earlier book (Knibbs, 2023).

THE OLD VIDEO GAME DEBATE: THE LITERATURE, WELL-BEING, AND MENTAL HEALTH

The varying forms of video game(s) debates have been eloquently described by several contributors within the space of digital media studies for some years now. I would suggest reading through the excellent, recent book that revisits the video game debate (for the second time) edited by Kowert and Quandt (2020). To give a summary of the book and the kinds of research that exist, I will give a small synopsis of the chapters because I am limited here by word count, but also I want you to read that book.

The chapters look at the research in-depth around each of these topics. This book on the other hand is a gentle introduction to whether gaming affects mental health or not and how this may or may not affect yours and leaves you, the reader, to investigate gaming research fully in your own time (if you should wish to do so).

LACK OF EXERCISE: THE IMPACT OF GAMING?

Initially in this section, I'll consider the issue of lack of movement and exercise in the population of 'gamers' (another nebulous term). It is interesting how often the narrative around gaming seems to ally with the obesity crisis and rising figures of health issues attributed to the sedentary lifestyle of the gamer. Images in memes or atop a mainstream media article portray the stereotypical gamer, usually a man in underpants, sitting on his sofa with food around him galore! Thus, gamer equals overweight. By now you are probably thinking, wait what about exercise sporting games as you mentioned above? And therein lies that dichotomy problem of 'what kind of gaming' equates to what kind of health-related issue? I wrote about this in my first book, about hikkomori, but even that is not enough of a literature base to say that gaming will result in health issues (Knibbs, 2023). That seems to be the exercise and health industries driving this mantra and narrative. And we certainly can say with lots of research sitting for extended periods is not great for our heath (Owen et al., 2014). And exercise can be a great tool for mental health, though this needs to be paired with a good diet and that appears in depth in my book (Knibbs, 2023).

ESPORTS, EXERCISE, AND EXTENDED SITTING HOURS

One of the biggest areas of gaming for extended periods would be esports (so it is said). There is a chapter by Orme (in Kowert & Qaundt, 2020) addressing this and the reason I'm tying these approaches together is because the domain of esports requires practice for gaming competitions in the same way footballers and tennis plyers practice for their matches. This might require extended times of gaming, and this may mean more sedentary time for the player. What is known about exercise and mental health together is not discussed in detail within the chapter. Therefore, when we think about esports you might have an image in your head of a young person sitting at their console or computer for hours and hours, and 'not partaking in outdoor play', which is what you will likely see reported on social media by news outlets and by some studies and literature in this area.

Mental health (and how exercise and diet can help) is a very big area of discussion outside of this book and Orme's chapter. What has been discussed by Orme in the chapter on esports regarding exercise is limited to games that are called exergames rather than exercise levels of gamers. Perhaps the misnomer between high-end mobile body movements 'in a gym, park or playground' as being proper exercise versus other forms such as exergames causes some of the confusion here when we talk about esports, as many people think it is a physical sport type game only. Again, it depends on the type of game being played at highly competitive levels and what this may involve, for example, Rocket League competitions play sitting down with a controller.

HIGH STRESS EQUALS HIGH ALLOSTATIC LOAD OR BODY BUDGET

What I can certainly say is that high-stress highly competitive environments require a lot of body energy (allostatic load (Guidi et al., 2020)), what Lisa Feldman Barrett calls the body budget (Barrett, 2018), and perhaps this is why many of the young people who partake in esports and elongated sessions of gaming that might be streamed live tend to be sponsored by companies promoting whey protein or caffeine-related productivity tonics, e.g. Red Bull and its connection with the high-stakes high-reward sports communities (Red Bull sponsorship: https://www.redbull.com/gb-en/energy-drink/contact-sponsorship). If you consider the amount of concentration required for extended periods of gaming, you would not be surprised to find that the highest consumer of that energy is the brain, which is required throughout the gaming process. Therefore, sustainable energy is often required in this domain and there are plenty of providers of such 'drinks and snacks' to oblige.

However, this is no replacement for real-world activity that is functional and requires the whole body. A further consideration here is when we think about Formula One drivers: they can also be seated for an extended period whilst engaging in minimal movements compared to, say, somebody who's rowing in a canoe or boat, and yet we know that Formula One drivers have a super high level of attentional focus on a seemingly repetitive task. Whilst there is more of the body involved in Formula One driving than sedentary gaming, I felt it important to add this as I don't see the same narrative surrounding exercise and Formula One that I do gaming.

Orme (Kowert & Quandt, 2020) even mentions the fact that esports competitors can also sustain injuries which often takes people by surprise, and there is a good reflection on health and taking care of your body if you are an esports competitor. There is also a new emerging space of 'biohacking and esports' (biohacking and esports: https://www.newhope.com/natural-product-trends/emerging-supplement-market-for-esports-has-high-score-potential) that go together in terms of sustained energy and sleep programmes using technology to become the highest calibre player.

When we think about mental health and how this relates to competitive spaces it will come as no surprise the esports competitors face the same challenges as people who take part in other forms of sport. I suspect it would be difficult to research the mental health impact of esports in the same way as producing a study of mental health in golfers, footballers, or snooker players, considering all the other elements in the players' lives that impact mental health alongside the partaking of the sport.

Again, it is a reflection on how we currently talk about this particular (e)sport and how at the time of writing it is not considered a sport (proper), maybe in the same way as people who play chess (who often sit for long hours when in a high-class match or competition)? Moreover, I wonder how the spectators of esports would be studied for their sedentary time and the impact on health. We don't often study people who sit down at comedy gigs or music events in this way either. I think they can be sat longer than the players at times!

If people are sitting for long times, and playing games to the level of global competition, is that a hobby, a career, or an addiction? This has been a dominant question in my head for some time, whether a video game player can be addicted to something that has the same foundational framework as a career in sport or a hobby. Yet within the 'screen time' debate, this falls under the gaming addiction or disorder criteria since extended periods of practice take place to the detriment of other areas of their life. For example, some children and some adults will not and cannot remove themselves from the practice (gaming) environment to carry out day-to-day functioning. This I believe is the same addiction David Beckham had as young football player.

So, looking at gaming addiction as a 'pathology' and this seems to parallel the regurgitated debate about gaming 'disorder', which also reflects the discontent between academics and clinicians as to how the addition of gaming disorder in the ICD-11 (World Health Organization, 2022) could be and was conceptualised.

And, how this is assessed in a generic and, or standard manner in practice settings. This has resulted in further delineations of what we now call 'problematic gaming' and recently (outside of the book writing process) I was introduced to the idea of problematic interactive media use (PIMU, Problematic Interactive Media Use: https://digitalwellnesslab.org/guides/parents-guide-to-problematic-interactive-media-use-pimu/). Much of the gaming disorder criteria that were produced by the World Health Organization for the ICD-11 uses the same lens as that with which we pathologise substance misuse, often called addictions, or where people have a gambling habit that is out of control and called an addiction too. One of the most fabulous things about the reflection on video game addiction is how clinicians (me included), argue for the contextual assessment and presence of other issues within a person's life that result in them retreating into a gaming environment. This can be for many reasons which may include a maladaptive coping strategy, compensatory processes, avoidance or perhaps this is a space in which they can communicate with others about their issue for support (Boccamazzo & Kowert, 2020).

For example, children may be questioning their gender and find some of the gaming spaces helpful, allowing them to manifest a new avatar, or talk with others as they work through their identification process. As there are no decades of long-term robust research on people who game and what impact this has over a long time, much of the literature focuses on what are called longitudinal studies of a few years at most (need I say a particularly short time within a person's lifetime). As is reflected in the chapter discussing this, Przybylski and Weinstein (2019) suggest it is episodic rather than chronic patterns of gaming. We do not have gamers who have displayed these patterns for decades in the same way gambling or substance misuse appears.

> Unlike the alcoholic who progressively drinks more over time, 'gaming' does not work like this generally.
>
> [my emphasis and reflection]

STREAMING, COMMUNITY, AND CONNECTION

An important reflection that appears in this chapter is the idea of a community space such as streaming live on Twitch or YouTube, and spaces like discord where people can congregate to discuss their favourite game or fandom about the game (or anything in general). People may find that they are required to play games, for an extended time, for a particular number of days in a row, for example to raise funds during the holiday season. One of the biggest (gaming) entertainment organisations in the UK 'The Yogscast' (https://www.yogscast.com/) streams live (for long periods) almost every day in December to raise money for charities. Members engage in gaming and conversations for an extended period of time per day, which may well meet much of the criteria for gaming disorder and addiction. But do they do this only once a year? No, The Yogscast have been a long-standing set of streamers that game daily, even more than once a day on some occasions as this is their employment/job or profession and probably something they all enjoy. (On paper this may look like a pathology, so when does it transition from a disorder to a profession?) They also have a large following, and the numbers of views they have in less than an hour of publishing a video on YouTube is testament to this. Those followers are spending their time on YouTube to watch the streams. They also spend time in online spaces talking to each other as a community. Is it the gamers (Yogscast) or the viewers who have a disorder? Because I suspect some of the viewers also game on top of the time spent viewing their favourite streamers.

VIOLENCE, CRIME, AND GAMING: A MORE DETAILED LOOK

Perhaps I should frame this as violent video games and crimes. Is this a link or a cause? This is perhaps the most contentious controversial and heated discussion that exists around gaming (Ferguson, 2010) (closely followed by the addiction conversation). For now we will focus on what has been said in the literature about violence and gaming, and much of this emerges from early studies around violent television and the copycat behaviour in children and young people because of a video experiment called the bobo doll (Bandura et al., 1961), which can be and is generalised to the adult population. Out of this literature emerged the general aggression model (Anderson & Bushman, 2018) and it's often purported to be the same mechanistic process behind violent gaming and violent crime.

In the book chapter discussing this topic Kowert and Quandt (2020) discuss the recent revision by the American Psychological Association (n.d.) towards the resolution of the topic of violent games and violent crime, providing the reflection that 'these are complex topics'. Przybylski and Weinstein (2019) produced a balanced reply to the existing research suggesting that violent video games do not provide a causal link to aggressive behaviour.

This is the first stop in the conversation around language and meaning again because *violence* and *aggression* whilst sounding like they are the same behaviour are not. When we look to adjectives and verbs to describe complex behaviour it can provide us with messy concepts and constructs which makes it difficult to study it accurately. Therefore, when we look at the categorisation of violence within a game and how this may manifest in the real world we often conflate many words that sounds similar. The variance on a spectrum of violence can include aggressive behaviours, but aggression does not always include violence.

BIG DATA

A piece of research using big data (another messy construct, but for now take this to mean lots of digital data collected over time) looked at large amounts of data taken from worldwide events, namely violence carried out by men in the real world (it's likely these are police/ security arrest and detainment figures). They found that when these men went to watch violent cinematic films that by default of them being in the cinema, usually in the evenings, crime rates of violent types reduced (Stephens-Davidowitz, 2018)! Often the correlation cited within sociological research spaces is alcohol increases the rates of violent crime.

I suspect you are shocked by this. Not.

HOW TO MEASURE VIOLENCE OR AGGRESSION

In studies that look at violence after viewing (or playing) violent material and in this case playing violent video games, participants responses after the game tend to use measures that are different from the violent game (Kowert & Quandt, 2020). These can be tests that measure reaction times, fMRI scans, classification of movements in the game (passive/violent), carrying out acts on other players afterwards that could be considered violent (loud noises played in headphones, taking imaginary money), or longer term surveys for example (Williams & Skoric, 2005). In other research gamers are measured cognitively afterwards (e.g. the Stroop test) (Kirsh et al., 2005). It is unethical to study whether a person would (actually) carry out a violent act such as hitting or kicking another sentient being, so we have to look to lesser acts of behaviours that we can call 'violent' in principle (suggesting it's the same brain and body mechanisms involved in the two kinds of acts), but it really isn't what we see in a violent act in the real world. It's all very confusing!

What is often misunderstood is a variation of aggression called frustration. There are so many forms of aggression, anger, and violence that we could be here all day defining each one. In today's gaming lexicon there is something called 'rage quitting' where the challenge and skill needed in the game is beyond what the player can manage, and results in disappointment and frustration and the sudden ending of the game. *This* is what parents report in my therapy office as being the problem, when the controller is thrown with a scream, howl, or rage noise. This can be attributed to the violence within the game rather than the difficulties of it, or perhaps how the game is made difficult by other players and or bullying, and why people may indeed exhibit rage, frustration, annoyance, disappointment, sadness, irritation, and the complete spectrum of sadness and anger which are emotional responses to something within the game environment. *It depends on the why*. I wonder how many parents, partners, or friends ask this question?

VVG AND REAL-WORLD VIOLENCE: SHOOTERS

In the book *Mortal Combat* (Markey & Ferguson, 2017) it's suggested that the school shooters discussed in the book did not play violent video games but rather exercise/music based ones, and were perhaps suffering with mental health issues which required the prescription of medication, some of which might have been antipsychotic in nature. The impact of medication on an adolescent growing brain is still in the early infancy of research as we don't know the full impact of hormones puberty and brain changes when they are steeped in medication. Mental health issues can be missed in this population by stereotypical suggestions of puberty, 'hormones', and 'typical teen behaviour'. Mental health issues in young people do not always look the same, some may disguise them, and of course we do not have enough trauma informed education systems around the world to identify childhood trauma as this is so often the foundation of many issues in mental health, psychopathy, and school shooters (Langman, 2009).

MENTAL HEALTH

And that brings us towards the idea of mental health and gaming, the impact of gaming on mental health, or as is often cited in much of the literature nowadays *well-being*. I will challenge what well-being is, what it looks like, how it can be measured, whether this is longitudinal, and/or is separate to all other impacts of everyday life. What might be considered for example, thriving, surviving, or well-being?

I'm not entirely sure what any of those terms mean when it comes to a robust measure of such language and constructs. So, when we see a complex construct like gaming having an impact on another complex construct we can see this chapter as being similar to the social media one.

We're looking at how a game (of many types), can impact a person, in the same way that exercise, sport, breathing patterns, meditation, nutrition, sleep, geography, poverty, social class, demographics, race, and gender have an impact. Research that looks at video games and well-being looks towards the same characteristics that appear when we start to see impacts on physical, social, emotional, and mental health. Kowert and Quandt (2020) in their chapter point towards some research and literature that suggests disordered, addictive, or prolonged video gameplay may well increase depression and anxiety. However, they show that other research suggests that these are the key elements to reducing or mitigating these types of issues. Thus, we have a catch 22 situation. What drives which? Furthermore, it is suggested video games impact self-esteem, life satisfaction, phobias, interpersonal difficulties, and hostility. They are as varied as the players I suspect.

It is also suggested that participating in games or by socialising promotes well-being, self-esteem, social competence, social identity, and more. Akin to the debates around social media and mental health in the previous chapter it is difficult to ever know if there is a causal link for either. Is it fair to say then that video games therefore are magical, they can *cause or solve* mental health and wellbeing issues?

Gambling, In-App purchases, and DLC

One of the negatives often associated with gaming is the gambling aspect (Griffiths, 2020). Downloadable content, or in-app purchases, might possess an unknown or surprising outcome. The most well-known of these 'surprises' are called loot boxes. There has been a fair amount of research looking at the connections between gambling and loot boxes and much of this follows the same thinking around gambling in the spaces of online communities such as gambling websites. It can use the same thinking towards in-game assets such as football packs for the teams in FIFA. Loot boxes are quite often called microtransactions in terms of extra assets towards the game, giving players an advantage or status. This is currently a way in which children in my therapy office, and probably lots of players around the world, exert their dominance, bragging, or status (via their avatar and the skins and outfits that these exhibit). These downloadable, purchasable, and risk-taking assets have been demonised and are often discussed in the same way as gambling addictions are.

The idea that loot boxes or the purchase of assets with an unknown outcome does indeed tap into what Griffiths (2020) suggests are the same mechanisms of gambling, where the player hopes that they can win something of value. He describes the mechanisms of gambling being similar to gaming and describes standard and non-standard gambling mechanisms. One of the areas that's quite often discussed is how the odds of winning are not always conveyed especially towards younger players, meaning the mechanism of 'I want to try again' can be provoked. If they do not receive something they consider a value and keep trying, then it's this process that is considered manipulative towards children.

And at the time of writing the UK Gambling Commission had previously considered loot boxes to not be the same as gambling, however a recent update in July 2023 (http://www.gov.uk/guidance/loot-boxes-in-video-games-update-on-improvements-to-industry-led-protections) by the UK government has convened a technical working group where they advise that the industry should not provide access to loot boxes to children, unless parents enable this (in settings for example). The chances of winning on the boxes must be communicated and spend caps are suggested too.

Within the chapter terms like problem gambling, gambling, and gambling style games do not make for easy interpretation when we think about the impact on the player and their mental health, or well-being, life satisfaction, and any other outcomes that we might discuss within this book. Much more research is needed.

Many more areas of study!

Sexism, harassment, cyberbullying, hate crimes, racism, terrorism, radicalisation, and gender related issues such as LGBQTIA+ are many more areas being researched all the time in academic spaces. They are covered briefly within some chapters (Kowert & Quandt, 2020), but not as in depth as chapters would be, of their own merit in Kowert and Quandt's version 2 book, so I suspect there are many more updates and versions to follow (I hope!).

As I end this chapter, the impact of computer and video games is still under study and to date the evidence can be both for and against any named issues. We have much more evidence to collate, and I hope for some standardised terminology in this space too.

NOTES

1 Platforms and genres: https://en.wikipedia.org/wiki/Video_game#Platform.

2 Games discussed in chapter https://en.wikipedia.org/wiki/Lists_of_video_games.

4

SOCIAL MEDIA, ADDICTION, MENTAL HEALTH, AND WELL-BEING: WHAT'S THE CONNECTION?

TWO SIDES TO A SEA, TWO SIDES TO A STORY

Studies in mental heath and technology and the great Atlantic debate(s): what I mean by this is important for this chapter because there are two sides to the story of technology and its impact on mental health and well-being and *neither of the sides in this argument or debate is correct*.

There I said it. No one has got this influence and impact narrative 'spot on' yet and I don't think they ever will because as I said at the start of the book it's complicated, multifaceted, and multicultural. Moreover, this space is like the weather in so far as we can't even predict that with accuracy. It is the same kind of system: *chaos* theory (Royal Meteorological Society, 2021) and applying online issues and spaces to human behaviour and well-being is like trying to determine weather patterns using a wet stone. We have an idea, we might be correct some of the time, and we can suggest patterns, but we are not accurate enough yet and perhaps may never be.

DOI: 10.4324/9781032617251-5

And this is science. We cannot prove it, we can only find ways to disprove a theory and right now how this research and sharing of information about online harm (impact on mental health) is being done is seemingly more about popularity, selling products and services, influencer clout (or ego), and the demonising of children – an issue with which 'technology' can be the bad actor or agent, as well as the child.

Neither side of the debate needs to be 'taking the other one out' because they don't like it or agree. But this is what it looks and feels like when you see these organisations, academics, and researchers on social media shouting at each other and dissing them in varying ways. From big organisations wanting to create a treatment plan, and films to be championed, to others wanting to be the best academics in the field and perhaps gain the assurance that they matter, are, and their metaphorical parents are proud of them. It's like watching children in grown-up bodies fight it out in the playground.

...and even this real-world physical fighting, was going to be an event taking place at one point with Musk versus Zuckerberg in an MMA-style battle with each other after several social media posts took place between them, like two boys in a playground setting up an 'after-school scrap' (Heath, 2023). Leading by example for our children here; way to go tech giants! (*Although at the time of writing the word on the street is that Zuckerberg said no to doing it; when the book is published it will be humorous to see what happened.*)

THE GREAT ATLANTIC DEBATE

The reason I call it the great Atlantic debate is because of the research I will now talk about and who/where this is being developed, shouted about, and shouted at, so to speak. It's an age-old battle of intelligence, refutation of others' work, and the production of new ways of thinking about the topic #science. Both sides have validity, and both sides seem to have a vested interest in being the correct 'truth' so I will discuss this here and remain neutral to the sides and keep out of the many complex analyses used in research (unless you are partial to algorithmic maths and statistics, in which case fill your boots in the reading of the studies).

This work has not been easy to read at times because whilst I trained in basic research methods as part of my academic studies, I am a qualitative '*talky*' person, clinician, and academic researcher. Rather than bore you with the minutia of the research I read for this chapter, I will be summarising it (and referencing it in the bibliography) so we can get to grips with it here minus the calculations. And herein lies the caveat of 'I might have missed some important elements' out of the findings and studies (I'm neither a calculator nor a prof in stats), so please bear that in mind as I am sure the analyst haters are going to hate that bit if it is true. I'm not using the lingo of the analysts as here I am hoping to explain to the public the research in a non-babble format. Fingers crossed I can do that accurately enough.

I find the online space of those sharing 'research findings' an interesting place where people, who often have PhDs, come down heavy on those who do not have a specialist degree and in understanding results and measures (such as chi-squared, anovas, and regressive analyses for example). The pomposity and hierarchy of research knowledge can often be on display like a peacock in mating season. This happened on the Joe Rogan podcast in 2019 when a film about veganism was trending (https://open.spotify.com/episode/110ulFKocbLDsLhZ0bJwwm?si=03acea4fa12446fa). One academic was literally and scornfully deriding and mocking another academic who did not understand 'box plots'. And, rather than explain this, kept attacking the other academic for 'being stupid'. I don't think any reader here is stupid, but you also may not understand box plots, statistics, and calculations used to assess validity for example, and who would want to, outside of academia?

As this is a book for the public as well as those with a research interest, that doesn't always include 'quantitative data' driven readers. I will explain the research in terms that even a child can understand (I hope) and instead of hiding fancy words and results behind 'research psychobabble' this may not be the easiest of tasks, but here goes…

RESEARCH APPROACHES: 'WOTS THAT THEN?' AND WHY SHOULD I CARE?

First; a consideration of the best 'type' of research to exist (so it is said) and that is called a *double-blind randomised control trial* (RCT) (Jones & Podolosky, 2015), where the people in the research and the ones doing the testing don't know what is being measured or why (only the people who designed the study are in on the secret, so to speak). This is so that nobody can alter the results by behaving or doing something to skew the findings. So it's blind to the people taking part, they are randomly assigned to the testing situations and groups and the researchers are blind to what's being tested for. It is a complicated process and often appears in medical settings, due to ethics and often because it is something ingested/injected (e.g. tablets or vaccines) that can be hidden (inside a syringe or capsule for example).

The 'thing' to be measured is quite objective, for example, in the hard sciences like physics, chemistry, or biology the item's taxonomy and description is agreed upon by the field and the ability to copy and redo the research can be easier as the studies focus is stable over time, for example, igneous rocks, water, or stamen in a flower. In human RCTs it is usually an objective measure of a biological process or outcome related to the experimental conditions, such as hBA1C levels, oxygen saturation, or chemical byproducts of the substance being tested or given to a person in the trial (for example I look for something called metabolites produced by the body when carrying out functional tests with my patients, and compare these with study samples of healthy patients that were discovered using these RCT techniques).

Social is subjective

This type of RCT research then is not possible for any research around social media. Not only because the internet and social media of many types now form a part of nearly everybody's daily life (much of the population of the world, on average 5 billion people, have access to the internet out of 8–9 billion people so that is a lot with access and without). But there are just so many things that can 'interfere' with the results (Bryman, 2001). And what do we *mean* by the term *the internet*? The field of academics here cannot agree on this definition, nor technology, nor social media, nor platform, nor app, nor device, and on and on. How do we measure something that is described differently around the world, and even within disciplines?

And so with this chapter taking a somewhat mirrored approach to the introductory chapters, there are so many types of social media apps, platforms, and processes that we cannot single one type out alone to measure. Moreover, to show the impact of the introduction of this 'tech' we would have to find approximately 3 billion people without internet connections (Internet World Stats, 2021) before they were supplied with the Internet or social media and then limit what they could access so that we could measure that specific behaviour unique to the introduction of social media whilst ensuring nothing else skewed the results. It is just not going to happen.

It was also a similar issue with the invention of the television. It might have been easier to conduct this kind of study because the numbers of TVs present in houses was smaller to begin with, the content was limited, regulated, and broadcast for a specific amount of time.

But TVs being present in homes did spark off some very interesting pieces of research about aggression and media (Murray, 1973; Huesmann & Eron, 1986), which are still cited today to create the link between violent media and aggressive acts later in life (Huesmann et al., 2003). This is often the reason why violent video games get the blame here too alongside racial stereotypes (often cited in the news when there is a massacre or catastrophic event involving weapons) (Markey et al., 2019).

I'm hoping by the end of this book you will have developed thinking along the lines of 'Well what kind of violence, what kind of game or film, how often, what do they mean by violence' etc. and so we need to put a critical thinking hat on for the rest of this chapter.

Atlantic storms

What we know about water and tornadoes is that together they are not a great combination. And, the space of whether social media is good for us or not and how it impacts mental health can feel a little like a storm has been whipped up with plenty of water and wind from many experts, resulting in a cacophony of noise, disaster, and some hope. I feel that the UK and the US are colliding on this topic mirroring hurricane season. The debris from the tornado is confusion and lots of 'expert' advice about these places and spaces, apps and mental health, well-being and not-so-well-being, and it is my job here to try and filter out the extraneous rubble and noise and present you with the objective data and results as best I can.

I am still storm chasing as I write this book and sometimes I get swept up in the wind and I don't have clear answers either, so I will provide you with the evidence for you to make up your own mind. If at the end of the book you want to err on the side of addiction, behaviours being a disorder, or a pickle that we are in (as I see it, an emergent behaviour of humans facilitated by tech spanning nearly 30 years with no guidance from the wise old folk of the village, hence the mess we are in) so be it.

I would hope that the thinking behind the thinking can be, in the words of a mindful approach to life 'a way to not get caught up in the wind and swept along with it'. Grab a brolly and boat (and maybe some snacks) as I have no idea which way the weather will blow for the next decade or so on this topic and we have yet to include the immersive spaces which are not being discussed, yet.

The studies, of what exactly?

The predicament of being able to read lots of studies and see a standard familiar lexicon was fraught from the outset. There is no standard language used by all the studies in the same way. Beginning with some questions I pose here for you to think about, when I throw into the mix, right from the outset.

Was and is *email* included in the studies about social media use and interactions? Does or did it include *video calls* and if so, how was this differentiated between work meetings or work-related or is it just when they are being used for calls with family and friends? What about calls to the GP in lockdown for example, how was and is this categorised? How was social media defined? What if some people don't use '*all*' of the spaces and platforms (apps/software) but only a few, what about just flicking through them passively versus someone interacting on every platform and having and interacting with conversation throughout the day? These are *just a few* of the questions I have.

These parameters were not always clear in the results, or the study itself. And this was and is still in much of the literature, ill-defined in the studies and books I read on this topic almost every week, and I am a culprit of using this language too at times.

What if the app being studied is in isolation, for example, the 2014 app 'yo' (Perez, 2014)? (This doesn't exist anymore, but all you could do before the update (Lomas, 2014) was send the word 'yo' to someone so it is a great example of being able to study the app's 'intention and use'.) Can we really generalise *all apps and behaviour?*

Elbows, kittens, or breaths?

Here is a thought experiment: how often do you touch your elbow per day, think about cute kittens, or how many breaths do you take when at work versus home? Could you accurately measure these things without either accidentally or purposefully doing more or less of them or even missing some of them when counting? (I'm sure someone smart will answer here – they would get a measuring tool for the breath counts!) And what about if you had to fill out a report on your count scores? Would you lie, exaggerate, or try to tell the truth, to try and look good to the researchers or to change the results of the study in some way by being a good student or a cantankerous one?

When I read the studies, these were the questions I thought about (and more) and how the participants answered the research questions or what their motivation or intent might be. When it comes to being a human, we tend to lie through lack of insight, not wanting to feel shame, wanting to brag and show off, deny or diminish a bad behaviour to avoid judgment (for example, GPs might be given answers much lower than the actual units of alcohol someone drinks because of shame and judgement (Britton, 2015)).

And how would researchers measure your truth-telling, or be able to make inferences about why you touch your elbow, why your breathing rate changes, and whether you really do think about kittens, or not, or just say you do? Complicated? Yep, it is. And so I say again: so is social media research. But patterns of behaviour and self-reported answers are usually the best we can get for these kinds of studies. When we look at past research, we must think about how the answers were given in that era. For example, the first studies about sexual behaviours were based on studies carried out in the 1950s (Kinsey et al., 1948/1998). It's only later that people felt freer to tell more or 'all'. Does this mean the 1950s' studies are rubbish? No, but it does tell us that things change over time, perhaps due to changing patterns of opinions and acceptance of certain things. The field of social media research is relatively new, but as the field moves so fast, we are often chasing the new platforms and adaptations (for example the introduction of infinite scroll or algorithmic feeds (Centre for Humane Technology, n.d.)). We can't compare apples to oranges but in this field we often consider all fruit equal. Which is a bit silly really.

THE HISTORY AND THE SETTING OF THE SCENE

Let's start with the approach that got us talking about this mental health and well-being link with technology. The early research, based in the US, was connecting dots from long-held survey data about the population of the country to post 'invention' of the iPhone

(Twenge, 2023). According to those studies it has taken some of the largest sample sizes of people in the US, reporting on a yearly survey, and behaviours concerning technology in that period before and after 2007 when the iPhone was available (Twenge et al., 2018). Some surveys studied by the researcher(s) were national and regarding a person's health, or numbers of hospital admissions, school attendance figures, and so on.

The researchers in this field are mostly social psychologists looking at the *collective behaviours of populations over time*. For example, how many self-harm admissions were there at emergency departments in the year x compared to y? Or what changing, emerging, or missing behaviours, statistics, or crimes were showing up in education, health, and policing, for example?

Based on these studies two professors, Jean Twenge (https://www.jeantwenge.com/) and Jonathan Haidt (https://jonathanhaidt.com/) have made a major name for themselves in this space with articles and books such as 'Has the iPhone Destroyed a Generation?' (Twenge, 2017) and 'The Coddling of the American Mind' (Haidt, 2019). You might be thinking, wow those are quite the phrases to garner attention, and you'd be right! This language is provocative and can prime readers as to what they might read in these books and articles. They lean quite heavily on what is often called victim blaming, shaming, or pointing the finger and they are soaked in what seems to be a conservative approach to the state of the world. This is not a political attack here, but one that is in direct conflict and opposition to the approach, findings, and conversations taking place in the UK as you will see.

These articles and books have some very interesting ways of looking at the rise of large population behaviours and how this could be attributed to technology, namely social media. For example, Twenge's article looks at the rising rate of self-harm admissions at the time of the iPhone (2007) and the time when she was comparing the peak rise around 2012 (Twenge, 2017). The curve is prominent and it is certainly worrisome to see how many young people presented with self-harm, but… why? The bit that is missing from the article (and the hospital records) because it doesn't get recorded at the emergency department is *the* **why** *of self-harm*. The story of the why, and the presenting narrative, is deemed irrelevant in most cases. The numbers tend to matter more here (sadly).

So all we have to look at, and try to understand is: what correlates with this behaviour? Lo and behold it's the introduction of the iPhone and social media as Twenge suggests, the self-harm is *because* of comparisons young girls are making about themselves online with other girls but this information is not collected anywhere in the admissions surveys and is perhaps a theoretical proposition with some evidence of girls reporting this (but I can't find this to corroborate). Now this '*comparison overwhelm*' is not an idea or supposition that lacks support or credence given the amount of research that has begun to appear citing social media or cyberbullying as a cause of self-harm or suicidal thinking in young people. A number of these studies are research articles that appear in the medical disciplines such as psychiatry or paediatrics (Brunner et al., 2007; van Geel et al. 2014; Memon et al., 2018). Also, some of the research in this area was and is carried out by Twenge herself, which is not a bad thing, but something to note.

Self-harm, social media, and adolescent trends, groups, and ideals are one thing and the separation of such things can be fraught with biases towards the connection between them, because in truth there is much more of this behaviour being recorded and discussed, and certainly in my clinic numbers have increased. I am more inclined to listen and lean into the story of why which I seem to hear more often, rather than comparisons to body ideals on social media or cyberbullying. I often hear about the difficulties in families and relational aspects there as a highly motivating and contributing factor to self-harm. I don't think this is being studied anywhere in depth at this time.

HUBERMAN, HUSBANDS, HYSTERICS, AND THE APPLAUSE OF A GOOD SHOW!

Quick tangent: there is a phenomenon known as social contagion (Ogunlade, 1979) which I (feel) think (and see) often dragged into this space (the term appears on lots of research papers) and this sometimes gets muddled up somewhat in the space of social media research due to the nature of its language and because it is a developmental social norm of wanting to be like everyone else, and is more intense for adolescents.

What is particularly interesting about this aspect of social contagion is that I see the term 'Huberman husbands' (Shugerman, 2023) being used on social media to denote those who follow health and wellness advice from Dr Huberman (2023) and are (in this case) the men who are now tracking and hacking their health, bodies, and lifestyle to be 'more' attractive to their partners (so it is said). And I haven't seen one piece of research yet that talks about this, what might be called a positive impact, in ways that use the addiction language. *Huberman podcast addiction?*

Strikingly when it is a 'positive' behaviour it often gets called a practice or habit… not an 'addiction' and Huberman's podcast is promoting learning (Malecki et al., 2019) which is how I want to place this language of social contagion here. It is neither good nor bad but a conduit to emotions (or behaviours) being shared among a population. For example, I want you to think about the time you watched a comedian, or a funny film, or just got hysterical laughs when with a friend or colleague and how long this takes to spread to the others around you. Think about how long you clap at an event when you hear others doing this action. This is social contagion too. Applause, applause!!

ADOLESCENTS, IN-GROUP EMOTIONS, BEHAVIOURS, AND IDENTITY: TRENDS IN iWANT

All characteristics named above are very important for adolescents. The social contagion theory is a little bit like a memory experiment I invite you to do here: think back to a time at school when you were aged between 11 and 17 and you saw another student with something, a physical item, a haircut, a sporting achievement etc., that you also wanted, and you were beginning to notice many others with this as well. For example, in the 1950 to 1990s baseball cards were popular (Jamieson, 2010), and so were Pokémon cards in the 1990s (Cook, 2001). But let's think about pop groups, identification, and rebelliousness which are also very important as part of adolescence. Do you know people who were labelled as punks, mods, rockers or emos or goths (depending on your age)? The pop culture and subsequent identification and developmental stages for many young people were often based on music choices with mobile music players such as boom boxes, Walkmans, and iPods (and occurred before the iPhone).

Was or is this called *teenage development*, *social contagion or trends*, *identity formation or in-out group behaviours*? Well, it depends on what discipline is doing the research. This adds to the complexity of what we are studying in the social media landscape because we currently have several disciplines looking at the impact and outcomes and subsequent language in the studies.

Nowadays any behaviour that has been seen on social media can be classified as social contagion if several young people engage in it, and we can call it trends, political development, ideology, peer pressure, culture shift, and many more descriptors (think about the gender debate and how this is talked about). And yet this behaviour has been prevalent in young people since the advent of them being in the same class, the same year, the same school, and even on the same transport routes to and from school. It didn't matter if a child was in the suburbs or cities, there was the feeling that certain groups of children, usually denoted as the *populars*, drive the popular motives of what I have called here the *iWant* trends, and even in the music industry we have a genre called this: *pop* music.

I have written in my previous books about trends that evolved from gaming (fortnight dance called 'the floss' anyone?) and we seem to look at these with a different light because they are fun and can become something of a family game too, so where there is no harm, we turn a blind eye.

VIEWING AND COMPARING ONLINE CONTENT AND WHY FEMALES SELF-HARM MORE THAN MALES?

How do we deconstruct this phenomenon of self-harm being associated with comparisons to online body ideals, or viewing self-harm content, and separate it from what is seen on social media, gaming, TV, cinema or video on demand? Or what is discussed in WhatsApp groups relevant to this? And why does the research highlight that this self-harm issue and body ideal affects young females more than males (Twenge et al., 2017)? Why is there little research looking at the why? And the conflation of these issues gets mixed up with the current changes of identity formation development and gender conversations. It's certainly a confusing space right now and I cannot see much clarity in this area and so am not going to delve into that deeply here, because I am struggling to make sense of the way in which the wind is blowing!

And yet, before the internet young people and adults self-harmed to regulate their nervous systems, and perhaps we didn't have as many discussions about it, but I can certainly see the admissions into hospital settings as a stark increase over time and the only answers we really have are how Twenge has made sense of the data. We didn't ask questions at the time and so we rely on what we can find in the data. It is this very steep change in admissions to hospital with self-harm that led Twenge to make the connection here. And it most certainly makes sense to think this way. This data is based in the US and is not compared to the rest of the world (that I can see).

SELF-HARM IS COMPLICATED TOO, IT DOES NOT ALWAYS CONCERN SOCIAL MEDIA

Presentations at emergency departments happen for several reasons. The harmer hurts themselves beyond what they intended (usually by accident, or using equipment that for example might have been sharper than they realised) and needs medical intervention. They are taken there by adults who want to help (or shame them). They can be dragged there by their 'mates' because it's a psychological game (Berne, 1964) (see my other books on this (Knibbs, 2022, 2023a, 2023b)), they need attention and comfort, they did it in a moment of rage or panic or to wind up someone else, they were attempting to end their life. It is attention *needing* behaviour and can often be part of group identity too.

Sadly the questions about the why do not appear on the numbers charts given out by hospitals as they are only figures showing the numbers and types of casualties and accidents that appear in an emergency room which could be a second, third, or even fifteenth admission and this fact does not seem to be reported in the data. The nuances of the why are missing and each why is always pertinent to the individual and is a history that is not equal to anyone else's in existence. If only we asked certain questions we might have more clarity on this subject. For now, it's the fault of technology, body ideals, and self-harm content (Kelly et al., 2018).

As I was editing this book I realised I had missed a big critique: that there is likely exponentially much more self-harm content, body-based images online, and influencers now compared to a decade ago, but I haven't seen an increasing spike or surge in the behaviours attributed in the 2017 article. There are no increasing rises in self-harm being reported around the world. So, the correlation originally suggested that young girls were seeing this content, comparing themselves by exposure to x numbers of images (in 2007–2012) and then attending hospital for self-harm related to these images and the internal comparisons they were making…

Then surely a decade later the same mechanisms would be at play in the developing child and the self-harm admissions would be even higher now in 2023 if this were true? Child development processes do not change drastically in less than a decade, so why do we not see an increase in self-harm admissions if the visual content creates a mental health impact resulting in self-harm behaviours? If it were true then, it should be true now. Have our young females suddenly developed a new superpower? And what about those who do not identify as female, or do?

Why the change?

THE OBJECTIVE MEASURE OF HARM IN SOCIAL SCIENCE RESEARCH

Looking at social media and mental health outcomes or related issues, how does the research *explain* this? Well, what is being measured and how? As we look at the research on self-harm as a topic it may not surprise you at this stage that much of the harm reported in studies is measured by versions of self-injury or self-imposed punishments(Knibbs, 2023). They are not explicitly called this in these studies but are referred to as eating disorders, disordered eating, orthorexia, body dysmorphias (surgery or aesthetics interventions), substance misuse, sexual behaviours, cutting, ligature use, burns, and ruminations or anxieties requiring medications, sleep issues, and suicidal attempts (Twenge et al., 2017) (see an entire book devoted to the topic of self-harm and suicide in my recent publications (Knibbs, 2023)). And so the question is: *what do we mean by self-harm in these studies?*

And *what is harm as defined by anything other than self-harm?*

When looking at the research about the impact of social media on mental health and harms, other items measured here include attentional difficulties, learning difficulties, cognition, brain volume, mental health diagnoses from the DSM-V (America Psychiatric Association, 2013) and ICD-11 (World Health Organization, 2022) (there are lots of these), language development, political ideologies, social skills, manual dexterity, and more. *What do we mean by impact on mental health or well-being* for example?

And *what are these harms and mental health issues compared to?* What is the 'thing' causing these outcomes? Perhaps teh interwebz?

MORE LEXICON = MORE FACTORS AND MORE REASONS!

All the outcomes above are measured against, to or from social media or problematic screen use, problematic media use (including interactive and immersive media), screen time, the internet, digital environments, devices, digital media, electronic media, online, screen media, gaming, and a host of other 'problematic' internet ready things.

Hundreds of factors, compared with hundreds of other factors, that could result in thousands of factors. If I were a betting person, I would put my chances on the lottery where I feel there would be more certainty in the outcome.

If you feel that the space of social media and mental health research is complicated, now consider what kinds of children and young people exist in the world and what factors may impact all the random chance factors I have just mentioned. For example, in these studies are we comparing biology, race, gender, age, socioeconomic status, geographical location, intelligence, disability, learning difficulties, and so on?

There is not one definition, measure, or outcome that is used in this research space consistently by researchers. I often see technology being compared to drugs and again I ask: what kind of drug, who for, what setting, what method of 'use', how often, what strength or even what is their DNA makeup in respect of these drugs, and so on....

In maths and physics the idea that we can predict weather is as close as we can really get to the truth of social media and mental health impacts. We are mostly guessing that it will be sunny, windy, or wet (and AI meteorology does far better than a human), and yet we will and do have to make daily and hourly updates (in our heads or using weather apps) as new changes occur and new emerging properties give us 'scattered showers, with a chance of sunshine, and a breeze blowing Mary Poppins your way'.

SO LET'S GO TO THE TOP: THE URGENT PUBLIC HEALTH ISSUE OF OUR TIME?

The Surgeon General in the US (Murthy, 2023) also looked at this 'urgent public health issue' of *the effects of social media on youth mental health*. He discussed this in May 2023 in an advisory document about the impact of social media on youth mental health, and this document says it has not been fully evaluated due to the lack of evidence as to whether social media is *sufficiently safe* (added for emphasis but what does this mean?).

The Surgeon General suggests that evidence indicates that there can be a profound risk to mental health, but this is not explained as to how. Aside from the suggestion, there are '*indicators*' (again what does this mean)? This is followed by the conclusion on the next page that social media has both positive and negative impacts (again not defined what these are) and this is corroborated by the line that 'the scientific community agrees on this fact'.

What is meant by any of these words or sentences?

Can you see how confusing these documents are and why they sound like scattered rubble from the tornado? It is contradictory throughout and emphasises that harms around self-harm are a worry, yet the evidence for this is still nebulous. And what do we really mean when we say children and youth *use this 'social media'*?

Even the US president suggested that he would speak about this topic during some rallies and events (although I'm not sure what he is adding to this) (https://www.cnbc.com/2023/02/07/biden-state-of-union-to-target-social-media-and-kids-mental-health.html). As I am not based in the US, I don't know what has been said there but I did see it on social media; more fool me for thinking that this could be/is/was true and taking place. Who is in charge of this debate and research and what is it we need to address as this public health issue?

I am more confused than ever now.

*Before heading to the UK studies for the same level of clarity. A quick stop-off in our cross-Atlantic travels to the island of *curiosity* (of) the language in this domain.*

BRAINS AS SOCIAL 'MEDIA' PROCESSORS

The first thing I would like to add here before continuing with the debate writ large in this chapter is this.

Why do we say the '*use* of social media' as though this is a different skill set of a human being who is social by nature? We talk about hours spent 'on' rather than 'in or with' others because there is media content. We don't 'use' the cinema, films, or TV. Probably because we are sitting still, not 'doing' anything to interact with the images with our hands, and we don't need to move the items by swiping on the screen to watch the next part, but we do *use a controller* to do that if we are '*watching*' our TV. See how confusing this can be?

Have we (scientists, researchers, journalists, academics, and professionals who have this knowledge) forgotten that our brains process information in a way that parallels media (the construct); we have an internal audio track 'running' (the inner ear as it is called (Baddeley et al., 1975)) and we have the (inner eye (Baddeley, 1997)), an internal minds-eye that can 'see' images that are both static and moving. We *are* media processors and so when we look at an image in the world, on paper, or via a screen our brain does a miraculous operation in working memory to understand the elements of that image (Logie, 1995), which will include the associative connections to similar images, colours, and perhaps even sound etc. *And* the information we have already encountered in the world for things we have already seen and understood, memories and more. This is a complex process involving the occipital and partial lobe, the limbic system, and the pre-fontal cortex all within milliseconds of receiving the stimulus of imagery and sound.

Why has the space of social media become so very muddled in our language of 'brain operations', and why do we refer to this as *using* it? Because our thumbs or fingers are engaged 'in' the process of holding equipment in our hands? Is it because those hand (thumb) movements imply 'use' like a computer? As I was typing this I was literally sub-vocalising the words I want to get my fingers to type, just like I would think about what I want to say, in words, in my head before speaking. I know I'm using a keyboard to communicate because I am typing to do that. So, how would you study my keyboard use and ability to communicate if you could not see the process inside my head, and how would you report this in research?

Furthermore, I suspect the word 'use' is common because we the adults 'use/d' the telephone, the kettle, and so on and so we think of the internet and devices this way and forget social media is a process of engagement based '*on and through* our social pathways', we are in it as soon as we touch the screen. This touching of the screen *to be with*, has missed the complexity of socialising and is seen as a function and 'use'. Yet, in the world of infant and parent, child and adult relationships we constantly touch the person we are having communication with both physically and metaphorically. Language is fun, isn't it! Especially in this field.

LAND AHOY: THE APPROACH OF BLIGHTY. SURELY THE WINDS ARE DIFFERENT HERE

Potatoes and horse riding

Back to the research and what is occurring over in the country I am writing from. Studying the UK's approach to social media and its impact on mental health is often carried out by cyber-psychologists, and much of this can be seen in the department of The Oxford Internet Institute (https://www.oii.ox.ac.uk/). Here you will find the crème de la crème of researchers, with a prestigious reputation and findings in the domain of social media and mental health that are counter to the US research mentioned above. This counterargument was the one that won me over initially (mentioned at the start of the book) as it supported my (at the time, desperately wanted) bias.

The mainstream media ran with some of this research using the comparison made in one study, reporting potatoes as being more dangerous than social media. This is not quite what was said in the research, however, it is now talked about in this way and will likely be known as the potato research from now on (Orben & Przybylski, 2019).

The UK has its own history of research comparisons that get taken way out of context. For example, other pieces of research reported in a similar way gave us the 'horses are more dangerous than drugs' headline. In the space of drugs/substance studies, Professor Nutt used a comparison of MDMA to horse riding accidents, head injuries, and subsequent deaths (Nutt, 2009). The article 'Equasy: An overlooked addiction' suggested (via the results) that more deaths occur due to horse riding than taking an illegal substance. This study resulted in him being sacked as the drugs Tsar in the UK as the government was (apparently) not happy with the reporting of the findings (or perhaps the findings themselves, who knows). We (the UK) are quite versed in using what some might call ridiculous concepts to make our point even though the comparisons are valid.

UK APPROACHES

The research on this side of the debate quite often takes large data sets too but differing ones from those cited earlier, and in some cases the same data sets used by Twenge et al. in their research. In this case, researchers carried out a detailed inspection of her methods, which has been cited as being skewed and biased (Orben & Przybylski, 2019). So here the researchers carried out other testing methods on these data sets and reported different findings (which I would expect doing different calculations).

Now to the untrained eye (which includes me and many academics I know), it is way too complicated for the average layperson to understand whether Twenge et al. or the UK studies were or are the most appropriate testing methods for these large data sets. How would we know which tests to use and why? So many of us choose (if we have a choice) to believe the reported academic rigour employed, especially if it is supported by pontification about the methods used when attacking each other. It feels like an art gallery guide suggesting their interpretation of a painting is the just and true opinion.

We must trust the scientists and academics. This can be difficult when results are reported in language we don't use ourselves or necessarily understand. If we revisit the types of studies that these are, or not, they are not randomised control trials in most cases. They are comparing concepts, survey data, and something numerical and report this to us *with vigour*.

And so the impression I see being shared for the public reader of these reports is that they diligently carried out the experiments and studies and are telling us the truth. We bow to the expert. But they are fighting, so whose side are we on? We look to science and researchers to tell us they read the results, and these are the truthful findings. However giving you this information here after reading many of these studies left me with a brain ache at a large amount of jargon, psychobabble, and complex processes that I had to decode.

I have included the research I read at the back of the book in the suggestions for further reading and references. Many of the public readers here, who are parents, who are busy people and don't have time for deep research readings tend to opt for '*Just tell me what it says Doc*' and do not question or have time to learn the intricacy of economics, statistics, and analysis. Read the hieroglyphs Cath and tell me what it says!

BUT LOOK, WE HAVE BRAIN SCANS, PICTURES, AND #FACTS!

More recently the debate has pushed more '*science-y*' ways of proving correctness and truth by using the approaches of brain scans, developmental tasks, attentional tasks, and more. A quick tangent (again). It is often the case that when the public sees an image of a brain scan they are likely to believe what is being talked about because we revere the 'labcoat' figure of authority and knowledge (see the early experiments by Milgram, Asch, and Zimbardo if you want to understand this compliance and fascination with adherence to Science, authority and more (Milgram, 1963; Asch, 1951; Zimbardo, 1973)). Moreover, the space of surgery, neuroscience and medicine has over many years posited that the people who work with brains must be the cleverest because it's such a complex organ, in the same way we revere scientists or astrophysicists. Whenever images of brains appear next to the study findings, we bow to this very quickly because we often cannot read the images, but they look magical! And we take the word of the person describing the complex, intelligent, and the way-too-complicated-for-you images and findings.

TANGENT: BRAINS ARE THE MOST COMPLICATED ORGAN IN EXISTENCE, AND WE KNOW LITERALLY A SMIDGEN ABOUT THEM

Brains tell us very little about who we are overall in the grand scheme of things, we think we know what it means when we see something happening in the brain (or not), and then we find out we know less than we thought because someone somewhere is an anomaly in this space and their brain doesn't do what that person did or does (Tuckute et al., 2020), and we have to rethink our approach (but often we don't).

We (humans and scientists) are obsessed with finding 'the' cause or brain area specific to human behaviour, thoughts, or processes but in reality, we don't know that much really. We certainly understand a lot for sure, but still, it's not enough. And I use brain science to teach and understand that 'in general, this area, is considered to be involved in x, y or z' but I know there is someone out there who doesn't even have this area of the brain and still can and does do what all other humans do.

So let's go lightly with the brain area scans meaning we understand all of this, especially in this field, shall we? Let's take it that they are *likely involved with, likely to give rise to and likely can be measured to understand something* but that is not the definitive answer to the why or cause of human behaviour. And if *we really understood the brain and its workings we ought to have solved, by now, what mental health is and how to help.*

MATURITY, DEVELOPMENT, AND ADOLESCENCE: WHY BRAIN SCIENCE ISN'T THE STANDARD OF ALL STANDARDS

The big help here is that we have concepts and some great findings over time, with an understanding that helps us; for example, talk about how children become adults, and what might be going on as they mature, and move through puberty. Neuroscience findings help us explain how something can affect a person (in general).

Science has used the concept of the *maturing brain in* adolescence (Siegel, 2014) and the idea that the brain changes (a lot) through the ages of 12o25 because there are lots of studies that say it is '*in general*' mostly within this time frame (Siegel, 2014). But we don't know exactly when a brain 'starts' to mature and move into 'adolescence' nor do we have the crossing-over-the-finish-timeline of becoming an adult either. Some children will start earlier, and some adults will finish later. We haven't got portable brain-scanning devices on children from the moment they are born through to adulthood, and how would we measure this anyway, who decides what a mature brain looks like or 'is has or does?' but we do say *a mature brain*...

So how can we say with authority that this type of approach (neuroscience) meets a particular standard for research? Are there normal brains (useless term?) and not so normal? Are there late or early developers, to and through adolescence and how do their brains differ exactly? And how, who, what, and where is this authority even in the discipline of neuroscience? Even this discipline argues about concepts and outcomes depending on the way it is measured and analysed. I propose that this will be a difficult task to find the clear cut, irrefutable evidence and yet 'here I am using it in daily practice' which irks my cognitive deconstruction of the science here! And so, back to the matter in hand, why is this relevant to the research on social media?

I am seeing research increasingly appearing in the domain of 'social media and mental health' that has brain science language in the title, or in the approach used in the study to cite expertise and fact (and possibly dominate with a 'high' form of science as discussed earlier). And what is being studied here exactly? The answer is mostly self-reported answers by the participants about their social media use and then a brain scan to confirm or compare something (Miller et al., 2023). To what?

My question is, what is the baseline being compared against? Even if it is an individual being compared to themselves, maybe a month or year ago, how exactly do you remove the (extraneous) variables of life such as those taking place between scans and stages of adolescence such as food eaten, beverages consumed, air breathed, exercise, toxins, pollution, stress, medication, geography, poverty or affluence, books read, TV watched, comics or games, jokes heard or told and museums, art galleries and cities visited etc. …

If the word on the street is true that *neuroplasticity is a* thing (Hanson, 2013), which is the word used to describe the brain changes taking place in response to experience, then just by the very fact that you are alive means that your brain is changing. By the end of this book, you will have a brain that possibly looks different from the one that started reading it! How is all this stuff being communicated to the public and why is the brain science stuff so popular in 'proving' that brains change in response to something? Why does this feel like the Wizard of Oz? Why is there no longform documentary showing how the brain changes in response to time spent in social media and what the participant was doing there? And how can we truly see the impact of something like social media that changes probably quicker than brains do?

Once the measuring tech catches up (portable brain scanners? which currently are terrible looking (Waltz, 2018)), we can have those real time films and studies, and the extraneous variables accounted for, and the definitions and behaviours standardised and knowledge of what is accurately happening in the brain, then we are all sorted and then we will have our answers. It might be AI that supersedes us here. In the meantime, let's look to some harms identified back on the other side of the sea through some more studies.

US: A LEDGER OF HARMS?

I mentioned several companies that are at the forefront of the conversation about technology and its need to be humane. Two organisations are leading this narrative, both evolved in the US and have used several high-profile people and platforms such as Netflix to create a documentary about the 'state of play in the world of technology companies'.

When you go to the websites of some of these companies and organisations you will find pages or areas on the sites suggesting that technology, namely social media, can have *serious long-term consequences* for the development of a person (child). To understand this let's break this down a little, starting with the language. The word *serious* creates a fear about what tech is 'doing' to the child.

The developmental harms under scrutiny on the page labelled as a ledger of harms are in research terms minimal over a minimal number of years (2014–2020, www.humanetech.com/). In the world of science, we require many studies to make large claims. The section on developmental harms has **12 peer-reviewed studies over a period of six years**. This is tiny. Comparably studies in nutrition for example for **one food such as broccoli had over 1,000 cited peer-reviewed studies for one year** alone (https://pubmed.ncbi.nlm.nih.gov/?term=broccoli&filter=years.2020-2020) when I conducted a simple search (using a broad parameters). This search was simple, not using specifics to filter or search all journals across the world for example.

> **So why is broccoli more important than children's development or mental health concerning social media impacts?**

NOTE: I am sure I would not (and do not) cite studies and theories in my work if I did not have a discipline of years of robust research to rely upon that has been pulled to pieces by other researchers and replicated many times to show this is a good study and reliable outcome. That would be irresponsible as a clinician, researcher, and tutor! So why are we doing this around technology and mental health, or children's development? Why the rush to believe in one study, one method, or one organisation? We are in the early stages of this research, and we need many disciplines to come together so we can take an overall viewpoint. Unless of course we are media outlets, selling our product or services, or to become famous and chase the clout.

DEVELOPMENTAL OR INCIDENTAL?

As a developmental psychotherapist, everything I do with my clients is about their development in varying domains of their life, from the physical to mental, emotional, social, language, and psychological and some other domains that I have specific training in outside of normal routes of therapy training. Yet the studies cited on this ledger of harms section of the webpage are so varied about what those developmental harms are (https://ledger.humanetech.com/). Confusion about these harms is quite clear as contemplation of suicide is not a developmental harm but a response to something, incidental or otherwise. The impact of cyberbullying was stated and cited in the research as being a driving factor for suicide contemplation so why is this being cited as a developmental harm, given the highest figures on suicide cohorts are men (in the UK) aged 50–54 (https://www.samaritans.org/about-samaritans/research-policy/suicide-facts-and-figures/latest-suicide-data)? We cannot use terms that are insufficient for the claims we make if we confuse them and misrepresent them in this way.

Other studies on the webpage, such as the ones about pre-schoolers, show deficits in brain areas for language. Yes, this is a developmental skill but also can be because of a lack of parenteral interactions (language skills) as they need to work more because of the rising cost of living over the last decade, or the number of staff in nurseries being less than optimal for the number of children present. Again, in the studies, it's the brain science 'thing' being suggested, but no comparable studies for the period of lockdown have been conducted where parents' presence is likely to have increased with young children, as well as their time on devices too (parents and children). However, there is a good study (Madigan et al., 2019) following children from two to five years of age and measures that they looked at in this research (one out of 12 good studies so far).

The research on risky behaviour post cyberbullying uses words like 'lifetime use of drugs'. My question here is, does this team of researchers have a time machine? The research is cited as being from 2017 and as far as I can see 2017 to 2023 is five years in the future, not a 'lifetime', so who are they following for these measures and how? When the study has follow-up data from the same individuals in 2077 we could say some of those things robustly. Moreover, in my line of work in therapy people who use substances often have many reasons for such use. Cyberbullying can often be a factor but not necessarily the ultimate cause.

There are also studies about alcohol intake, unhealthy food, influencers, and the 'use of media before bed' (daytime *and* evenings), but *not during the night*, as being linked to depression. No studies on gaming? Are these studies citing incidental responses, or revealing how a human self-regulates, or providing evidence of actual developmental delays? As a therapist in this space, I am struggling to see how some of these are linked. When reading the research, to my lack of surprise, many of the studies are conducted in the disciplines of paediatrics/medicine which have not taken a truly developmental approach, but a symptomatic medical one. I did not see much written about how the delays in development occurred *because of social media*.

My favourite cited research on the webpage is the study on memory decline that assesses 25–75-year-olds and found that memory declines with age, who knew? I jest, *that's not quite what it says*, but it is a study that assessed memory after using social media. The abstract reads that the relationship between social media use and memory might just be… exacerbated by age-related declines in… memory recall. More social media use resulted in people having memory recall problems on the day and the day after (Sharifian & Zahodne, 2020). The study was conducted in the discipline of gerontology (older human beings). The space where we know that 'brain farts', 'brain fog', and neurodegenerative diseases (Alzheimer's, Parkinsons and degradation of brain matter) are associated with the ageing process (https://neurodegenerationresearch.eu/what/). That's the whole spectrum of development covered.

Discernment and critical thinking matter as much as your (brain) matter matters.

One study does not make a theory and broccoli, clearly, is more interesting than the ledger of harms that technology may be causing humanity. Take note AI… we care deeply about sulforaphane!

THE SPECTRUM OF BEING HUMAN IN SOCIALISING: NEUROTYPICAL AND NEURODIVERSE

These terms are becoming quite popular in everyday language and are often associated with attentional and social pathologies (ASD/ADD/ADHD) where rates are increasing (https://www.cdc.gov/ncbddd/adhd/timeline.html, https://www.cdc.gov/ncbddd/autism/data.html).

Is this social contagion I hear you cry (if you have been thinking critically about this set of studies and can see that increasing rates must mean that social media is at the helm)? We must discuss this, as many of the studies so far in this field of social media omit the variances in human social skills in the studies of social media spaces. There are no brain scans to show us the differences in the spectrum of divergence, especially when socialising on the platforms (and yet we know there are differences in the way people socialise that are neurodivergent).

OTHER OMISSIONS

Moreover, the space of gender identity and development is also said to be increasing with many genders being named, and *this is* blamed on social (media) contagion (Shrier, 2021). It's like we can pick and choose what we do or say with these concepts, when it suits.

Even with these two concepts, there is no robust way to differentiate these via a brain scan (that I can find), and so is the data, or are the studies, taking account of how social media can impact a person with neurodivergence and/or gender fluidity, and where on the spectrum are they measuring them and what against?

So, it's the survey-type data that will help us the most here. Furthermore, neurodiversity is also a spectrum and is different for every single child and adult I work with, and this takes us back to that comparison of apples and oranges (in Spain and Australia in Autumn and Spring). *We must get better at inclusive research* (there is some emerging) that can help us identify areas of change or interest and *we must share this research in ways that the public can understand easily*. We must also include lots of the factors that might seem moot at this point. Broad thinking here is going to mean lots of data points and *that requires the big tech companies to help* (that might have been a moot point).

DIVERSITY IN THE STUDIES: WHY UK VERSUS US SHOWS VARIANCE

Much of the research in the UK has found counterarguments to the US and because some of the researchers are in slightly differing fields using differing types of data, with differing sets of people I would expect to find differing types of studies and results. *We must do better at working together*.

MORE STUDIES AROUND THE WORLD, PLEASE!

Lastly, I would like to see some research on populations that have technology and maybe use it in different ways. What about those who do not have individualised cultures, like those who appear in much of this research? I wonder how populations such as Aboriginals, Himba might compare?

BUT This Research Is Not All Bad!

I am critical in this chapter to make a point. As I was writing this chapter, I kept thinking that readers would be throwing the bath water out and never taking research seriously if nothing can ever be 'proven' (this word only applies to dough anyway). The section here introduces the idea of critical thinking in the space we call the social sciences. Until we have more data from the big tech companies with which to follow the breadcrumbs, we are pretty much reliant on the public telling us what they can do, can't do, don't want to do, totally want to do, lie about, and exaggerate in surveys and find a way somehow to compare this to a baseline.

It is absolutely clear that the human race is changing with this technology, and sadly by the time this book is out the world of AGI may be upon us which is going to create another pivot for sure (Chat-GPT4 and Grok are already streets ahead in the space).

How social media impacts us is a difficult space to ignore and to get quick enough results is hard. The platforms and places children can go change rapidly, what and how they communicate, what happens there and how that can help, or harm, is just as fast too, but children's development has not really changed over time. There are some changes and those are about *managing human interaction in a way that we have never had to encounter before.* I would love to see more in this domain. This is sadly where I see the research deficit the most.

Much of the research from the UK has shown that it's a two-way interaction of impact and behaviour. Emotions and feelings can drive time spent in those spaces and that can either help or hinder *or* time in those spaces can help or hinder emotional responses and *that is what has the impact on mental health* (Lopes et al., 2022).

THE CORPOREAL WORLD, HOW MENTAL HEALTH EXISTED AS A RESPONSE TO THE WORLD BEFORE TECH

Our daily emotional valence can drive our proclivity to engage with the world or not, and our engagement within the world can drive how we then feel about the interactions we have (or lack of). A human being 'in' social media is looking for a *need* meeting or to meet someone else's needs. A human being 'in' social media is attempting in some way to engage in social behaviour. And that behaviour can be positive, toxic, or even banal.

> ***Broad brush strokes do not provide the fine detail needed for a complex exquisite painting and this domain is nebulous, ever changing, like the clouds.***

5

HOW CAN I CHANGE MY HABITS AND GAIN MASTERY OF MY TECHNOLOGY USE?

WHAT CAN HELP ME WITH MY TECHNOLOGY? USE, ADDICTION, PROBLEM, FEAR, PARANOIA, DOOMSCROLLING, AND MORE

The most frequent question I hear from people who attend my therapy clinic when they have a problem or issue, sometimes with gaming or social media, is:

> 'Will *it (therapy)* help or can you help?'

I can help them find a solution through the process of inquiry and exploration. We work together for them to action the changes. This chapter is a version of that thinking and process. *It is not clinical assessment, treatment, or medical advice.*

Questions and reflections about technology (over)use that appear in the room are quite often based on an article they have read or a generic understanding of pathological language such as depression, anxiety, or addiction (when they may not meet the clinical criteria for these disorders). Now many of the people who attend therapy do not say the word disorder when they describe their issues and would

DOI: 10.4324/9781032617251-6

likely be mortified to think, describing their symptoms to me, that it could be called a disorder. Many say

> 'It can be bad at times, or it is bad, well it's not *that* bad'.

Therapy language has infiltrated the everyday space (especially words like narcissist, gaslighting, and addiction) due to the prevalence of its usage on social media. Hardly anyone in my clinic wants to be diagnosed with a disorder but would like a *description of the problem*. Sadly, everyday folk won't necessarily know the differences between generalised or specific versions of the diagnostic criteria, or what that could mean in turn for a 'treatment plan'. Many do not carry the DMS-V (American Psychiatric Association, 2013) or ICD 11 (World Health Organization, 2022) in their pocket.

So how would I treat a person who said they were addicted to their phone, social media, gaming, technology, TV show, particular platforms, or the time on devices? Time spent for the work they may need to carry out, at all times of the day, what we call the 'workaholic'?

How can I *treat* the reader here (as in treatment)? The answer is I can't because I don't have enough information about them, their past, and other elements of their problem or whatever they want to call it. I can lay out some ideas about how I would work with this clinically and add in some directions for the reader. That is all I can do in a book, with the caveat warning that:

> NOTE: *This is not medical or treatment advice, nor can I or the publisher be held accountable for any undue distress that may be felt by the reader if they choose to carry out some of the tasks mentioned in this book. The help of a professional is recommended more than once throughout this book, and this is again recommended here.*

WHAT WOULD CATH DO?

I would likely start with a process of gathering a subjective, objective, historical, and medical history. If possible, I gain insight into the person's background through their storytelling and some measures of information gathering that is not included here (specific to the issue). When this is a young person, I tend to work with the adults surrounding the children's lives, by calling on family, education, and social care if they are involved and I would spend some time looking at a person's development from two generations before (when I can get this info), through to in-utero (womb) development, early childhood and to date. The luxury afforded here is my profession gives me time to explore this, and many years of working with trauma to know how significant each of these domains is in understanding a person and their behaviour and what interventions to 'use' for what a presenting issue might be for example, 'excessive doomscrolling'. *It is rarely ever 'just' the presenting problem that needs addressing*.

A problem with or around technology, gaming, or social media doesn't *just arrive*. Childhood matters in all aspect for both children and adults. That is where my first book comes in (Knibbs, 2023).

It is *why we all do what we do* in the space(s) technology affords us to visit.

I shall not recount the whole of that book, but safe to say I will give some helpful guidelines for you to consider and take away to work with, and I suggest you read that book too. As with the Instagram gurus giving you a meme or short video to heal yourself, this synopsis does not do a great deal more than give an overview. There is nothing like a great professional to help you work out where you may need to change, tweak a behaviour, or work with your past. And yes, some of the AI bots that will be, and are available to help you do this will likely be a good enough substitute because after all, they train themselves on hundreds and thousands of memes, glib sentences, and great books. Let's hope they don't try to sell you supplements, diets, or programmes though!

Everything they assimilate and decode is based on years of Internet data provided by those using the space and of course, copyright doesn't seem to matter here either. In fact, in Chat GPT's early days,

I asked a question about Cybertrauma, and it gave me my last ten years' work summed up in a few sentences. I have been blogging, vlogging, and podcasting for a very long time on this subject matter so it was rather funny to see how this product summarised my work back to me, although truthfully I am not sure how I feel about it. Yet.

SO WHAT DO WE GET 'FROM, IN, OR THROUGH OUR DEVICES'?

I gave a TEDx talk (Knibbs, 2022) on the why and how, and when we engage in behaviours in and through our devices. We often use our phones, computers, consoles, or devices to meet a need. This need likely has its roots in childhood that were not fully met. What Bowlby (1997) would have called deprivation (the other end of this spectrum is privation). Now parents do not (necessarily overall) mean to deprive their children of many things, even those who look to the outside world as cruel, punishing, and do deprive their children purposefully. It is often a belief that this is a way to educate and train their child (supernanny is an advocate of this model and way of thinking). Or it is an unintended consequence of poverty and trauma.

Nevertheless, some parents unknowingly deprive their children of the most basic needs of presence, attunement (think resonating tuning forks here), attachment, and co-regulation.

To make this simple: we need our parents to notice us (when we are tiny through to today even if we are 75 for example), and to attend to our sounds, facial cues, words, and body language. We need them to revel and marvel at our existence and not place any motives or conditions to receive this love, care, and attention. In my book I quote Dan Siegel's four Ss here which are, we need to be safe, seen, soothed, and secure (Siegel, 2023).

Well, it turns out not one of us gets all this, all the time, and so we find ourselves continuously seeking this from *other* people we meet along the lifespan in varying ways. *This is what it is to be human.*

ADDICTED TO HAVING NEEDS?

So when I hear questions like 'Am I addicted?' Or 'I am told I am addicted to…' I tend to take a moment.

What does the person want to hear, what do they need to hear and what need needs to be met? Those *needs* of ours are the ones exploited by the technology spaces.

WHAT'S THE CURE?

I wonder if you are frustrated that I haven't given a ten-step 'cure' yet? There isn't one sadly, although there are things that you can do to work out what is being exploited in you (or others) and this gives you a/the power to make choices. *That is your game changer*. So let's look at some of the needs that people have. You might find there's a number here that you identify with.

Love (there are six types: Eros, Ludos, Storge, Agape, Mania, Pragma) (Sternberg, 2008)
Empathy (not sympathy or pity)
Undivided attention
Friendship
Self: worth, esteem, meaning, identity, or image
Connection and community
Safety (psychological, physical, and emotional)
Autonomy
Play/fun
Authenticity
Goals, aspirations, and purpose

And other characteristics you might see listed by Maslow's (1943) Hierarchy, but I prefer the Kaufman (2020) sail boat metaphor as it's a continuation towards self-transcendence.

If these needs are not fully met because the people in your life cannot meet them, for any number of reasons, or you chose not to 'let them in' so to speak… then the tech companies have the upper hand. And this is where the following awareness exercises and subsequent choices can help you slow, stop, or prevent those 'excessive', difficult, or problematic (to you) behaviours.

> *Constant scrolling. Looking for something that can't named… could it be a need?*

WHY CAN'T I STOP? BECAUSE TECH COMPANIES DON'T WANT YOU TO!

I wondered when writing this book whether people would come straight to this chapter to help them manage their use of technology, social media, or gaming. I will never know the answer to that and so this chapter was written with the guessed answer of 'yes' in mind.

INSIGHT AND MODELS THAT CAN HELP

When therapists work with a client in the room (child or adult) they might be given some information (psychoeducation) about *why* they are doing what they are doing. For example, they may be given some neuroscience findings, some theory about human behaviour, or a discussion about how many other people have been in a situation like them. This is what therapists call normalising a behaviour, for example, lots of people who attend therapy have thoughts that can be overwhelming. And, many people who do not attend therapy can have these types of thoughts too.

I might share with my clients that people in general can find times in their lives when thoughts become dominant, they cannot switch off from them and they ruminate a lot. This might be explained and explored using the framework of mindfulness, and how watching our thoughts can help us see them as being like clouds passing by (Harris, 2015).

Some people might want to delve deeply into the why and others ask, 'How do I make it stop' and don't want any background knowledge. Both approaches are offered here (as much as we can know why we do what we do) and some tips for being able to lower, reduce, or control your tech use; and no, I won't be advising a detox, camp, or abstinence, unless you want to. I would like to offer solutions backed up by lots of theory and interventions from the trauma space. I don't believe social media or gaming warrants a 'detox' protocol, like (substance) detox clinics offer because you can't avoid these spaces for the rest of your life, and you would never see this model used for eating disorders (we know abstinence kills).

That would be like saying abstain from human interaction and we know that does kill people, it's even got its own label, loneliness (Heinrich & Gullone, 2006).

If you skipped the science chapter then step one of insight is: you are the equivalent of a lab rat as far as most of the tech companies are concerned and they have so much 'insight' into your behaviours, wants, and needs that you never stood a chance, *till now*.

EXPLOITATION, SHAME, AND THE BEHAVIOURS THAT FOLLOW

Many of my clients have been exploited in some way, shape, or form as they are either children, have been in unhealthy relationships, or have traumas that involve deceit, exploitation, and coercion. If we quickly go back to the list of needs, what happens when we do not have those needs met are usually some if not all of the following *emotions*:

Shame
Loneliness
Despair
Distress (depression and or anxiety)
Anger (fury, rage, frustration, annoyance, irritation, etc.)
Helplessness
Hopelessness
Sadness
Confusion
Emptiness
Disappointment
And more…

And what does a person do when they feel these emotions? Mostly in this case for this chapter, *they reach for their device to find someone or something to help alleviate these feelings*. And that is when the vulnerability can be exploited to its maximum.

A behavioural action is intended to soothe the emotion and often it can lead to a circular process with an accompanying thought gremlin confirming the feeling. The person is looking for the pain they feel to *go away*. Often, we seek this through a behaviour that we engage in to distract us from the emotion or thoughts.

CBT, DBT, OR NLP IS THE CURE!

Whilst not my primary therapeutic modes and so I may be seen as smirking at these models, this system of Cognitive Behavioural Therapy (CBT) (https://www.nhs.uk/mental-health/talking-therapies-medicine-treatments/talking-therapies-and-counselling/cognitive-behavioural-therapy-cbt/overview/), Dialectical Behavioural Therapy (DBT) (https://www.mind.org.uk/information-support/drugs-and-treatments/talking-therapy-and-counselling/dialectical-behaviour-therapy-dbt/) or Neuro-Linguistic Programming (NLP) (https://anlp.org/knowledge-base/definition-of-nlp) can help *some* people with the breaking of the cycle mentioned above. These are often models used in primary healthcare settings and often they are short term interventions. Feelings, thoughts, and behaviours are quite often drawn as a circle (or whatever shape is used) of being a human. We have needs in each of these domains and each one drives the others. If you can 'break' the cycle you can often change the outcome of one or two of the other domains, because they need each other to 'work' and reinforce the process.

However, what often happens for the people I work with who previously tried these modes of therapy intervention is 'this is a temporary fix', or they find themselves repeating the cycles months or years after. I am often told that it was helpful 'but, it didn't quite hit the spot' and 'there's still a feeling lurking that I can't quite get to or resolve'. It would depend on the practitioner and the problem, but childhood trauma often needs an entirely different approach and insight isn't quite the be all to the end goal.

A phase that might sound familiar to you if ever you have known someone trying to quit a habit, behaviour or addiction is 'I found myself thinking I could manage it'. They (CBT, DBT, NLP) *are* helpful for some people so this is not a bad rap, but it might not get to the core of what we are discussing in this chapter which is the (often) deeply hidden (but known) feeling of *shame*.

I FAILED. I AM BAD

What is this thing you are trying to manage? It is said by many the pop psychologists that recurring behaviours (addictions) are because the thing (nicotine, alcohol, drugs etc.) has a hold over a person, and they don't understand the power in the substance. They can't help themselves, it's a disease, it's in their DNA, it's hereditary, it's inevitable and so on...

But. What if it was that they didn't understand the driving force behind the behaviour. Even if they did know what the driving mechanism was, just knowing about something rarely stops the behaviour.

This is why I want to emphasise here that the insight I spoke of earlier is one piece in the puzzle and you need the corners, the sides, and the middle.

PUZZLE PIECES, AND AWARENESS

Let's start the puzzle with the corners as most puzzles are four sided (this is because this metaphor only works for that shape I suppose). This is *beginning with the identifiable parts*. And this often means describing behaviours that a person engages in, because lots of the people including children in my clinic have issues with naming emotions or the thoughts that surround the behaviours (so only anecdotal evidence here!).

When clients do name a thought, it can be the start of a longer chain of thoughts. When you follow the breadcrumbs, it leads to a *need and the emotion that sits with it*. To give you an example:

Margaret often complains about the amount of work she has. She finds saying no to people difficult and as a result ends up with lots of stress because of the things she keeps taking on, especially when she is busy!

In a systematic flow here, you can follow the simple interpretation (*very simple* and doesn't account for all needs, behaviours, emotions, and thoughts).

Margaret says:
'I didn't say no to making the cake'... (insert whatever behaviour you want here such as working overtime, playing taxi, staying up late, going to the opera)

Which means:
'I was worried about offending them as they have an important job and are my boss'.

Because 'I don't want them to be angry with me'.

Because 'when I was little (under seven) this feeling (anger towards me) meant that I had done something wrong and would be sent to my bedroom'.

And that means 'that I would be alone'.

And that 'feels frightening'.

And a memory feeling now appears:
Because 'my parents would punish me in this way in the past'.

And 'I would feel like I was bad and had caused them to be angry with me because of my badness'.

So 'I can't say no and that protects me from feeling afraid, lonely, scared, bad, shame, avoids conflict (which I don't like) and I feel in control (sort of)'.

But really 'I am feeling powerless and angry, and I want to have a say in what I do or don't do'.

So 'I will take that anger and use it in a way I can control, which is to complain... A lot!'

and I feel terrible for moaning and whining at you, the person I shouted at... etc.

This is shame, rejection and is often what happens to young children. They often don't get a say in much of their lives. This 'badness' may not be true as a fact... *but the child feels it is so and so it is.*

I wonder if this rings true for some of you reading this.

Be = Cause. What is the link?

So, breaking the cycle can be much more about the deep wounds and feelings which lie far beneath the surface of a behaviour, thought, or emotion. If you had to write out your behaviours, feelings, or thoughts in the example above, I would invite you to add 'because this/that means or leads to...' and see what you uncover.

You might not be surprised that at the end of the exercise you have written something like: I am bad, I am unworthy, I am lonely (I have no one), I am worthless, I am useless, I am angry, I am powerless, I am overwhelmed, I am disappointed, I am distressed, I am....

It's likely to be one of those feelings discussed above when a need goes unmet. You will likely have heard, or remembered sentences uttered by adults in your past. The truth of the matter is *these are quite often the opinion of someone else, not a true fact*. That's an opinion of someone else not a fact. But boy do they feel like a truth!

NEEDS LEAD TO...

If you are not getting a need met by someone in the real world, say your boss, your teacher, your partner or whomever, then you will go looking for that need to be met elsewhere. The feeling you have is likely tied to your childhood at some point and that can mean it is often a feeling that you are so familiar with that it is supersonic at presenting itself in your life. Whapam! So when it appears, you are unbelievably quick to do something about it and you beat the sound speed record in taking action. Quick, pick up the phone and find someone or something to ease the pain!!!

This process is much deeper than many of the substance dependencies people have because this is a primal action, and behaviour to get a need met (not the picking up of the phone obviously but the intent behind it).

This is not an addiction, this is about human beings wanting, yearning, and literally having a *hunger for* connection (Berne, 1964) to another human being. This is why putting the phone down is an arbitrary measure for a short while, and why many of my clients cannot 'detox' from being human. The clue has always been in the title of *social* media, and gaming has many of the same facets when it is cooperative, shared, and online because you are connected often in some way to others in this process (see my previous writings for an in-depth explanation on this).

COMMUNICATION AND THE NEED IT MEETS

Think about how many calls (during the week or weekend) you have watched your parents, or any adults receive from an elderly person such as your grandma. You might well see the 'dependence' on the adult (your parents for example). The calls? Well they can be about peripheral issues such as who was at the gardening centre today, what the weather was like on Sunday, what colour shoes Margaret or Philip wore in church, who is getting married, who has died and so on and so on...

How would you describe Grandma? Would you use the word addicted to phone calls? Or might you say lonely? Might you say anxious, worried, or would you even say 'needy'? So why is *this form of communication* and contact seen in this way and not through a lens of addiction? Babies are born to be social, if they didn't, they would die through the process of rejection and abandonment. If you can't connect with other human beings, you will literally 'starve' and this is why in Transactional Analysis it is called a hunger, because it must be satisfied.

> *You cannot take extended fasts from your connection hunger. You cannot detox from something that satiates, which can be nourishing if it is the 'right' food group, but you can detox from the toxicity of unhealthy relationships and the behaviours that go along with this.*

Most importantly for this part of the book:

> *What can you do to help you with your social media and gaming 'diet'?*

There is a likely helpful metaphor of a diet here, and this is why a colleague, Jocelyn Brewer (http://jocelynbrewer.com/digital-nutrition/) uses the framing of digital nutrition. Which is the time you spend on, doing, and interacting with technology and comparing it to the level of nutrition it provides.

DETOX FROM POISONS?

If we look at the food metaphor and consider what's poisonous to all humans and only poisonous to some we can think in the following way. What can be ingested or imbibed and what cannot be tolerated? What is toxic? In this section I invite you to think about the *content* rather than the time when we consider what is toxic and what you could detox from in this respect (I am aware this sounds like a contradiction).

I would ask that you consider your primary needs for these lists and those think/feel/do processes so that you can design your #yes-go and #no-no food-types, as in what you will engage with or not (gaming, social media, or drama in those spaces), and how you can think about the time you spend in or on those spaces. By this I mean the following example:

My **#yes-go** list is

When I feel
When I am
When I have

And for each of these I might write out something like:

When I feel: in a good mood, happy, secure, safe
When I am: at home, after meetings, have no time demands from others (e.g. be online at x time), not eating whilst…
When I have: time (at least 30 mins to play with), my battery level (over 40%), when I have nothing to urgently by (a spending cap)

And my **#no-no** list is

When I feel: angry, tired, bored, frustrated, lonely, sad, pitiful for myself, wanting to distract away from a person (post argument with them or to avoid an uncomfortable conversation)
When I am: in school, class, meetings, on the bus, with a partner or child, out for dinner
When I have: no money, or just been paid, when I want something (called retail therapy), I just saw an advert for something, no patience, little time, between appointments, just before going into the doctor's surgery and so on…

Hopefully you get the idea. Your list will be specific to you, and you may even have some other categories. Hardly any of the ideas on this list are surprising to me and I break a number on my #no-no list when I consciously chose to, or I forget because I forgot to do the 'check in' with myself first. This can be a big learning curve for many of us, because what we are often doing is: turning on the console, PC or opening the phone without doing a little 'self-check in' to see if any of the above criteria is present or not.

SELF CHECK IN AS A HABIT

How do you get to be aware of your phone pickups, your console, or keyboard clicks and immersion into the space of technology, games, social media, news, banking, drawing, reading, sports updates, health apps, timers, and whatever else there is on your device? Read on to find out.

HELPFUL STEPS IN USING THE SAME TRICKS BIG TECH HAS IN ITS ARSENAL!

Create an image or icon to tell yourself to check in, that you display on the case, locked screen, screensaver, covering the camera or On button (you would need to print a small image/icon to do this) and use this like a safety check sign that you may need to change every day/week (or hour) depending upon how quickly you begin to ignore it. This is why pushes and pings only work for a short time if we don't make them a part of daily practice. The suggestions are 21, 30, or even 90 days depending on whose work you read (Clear, 2018).

Now you might not know this new habit-forming time for you. But you need to have a different mindset towards it, for example think about the alarm clock snooze process; many people set an alarm to ignore it! So you have to make this an *active choice*, what is called a nudge in behavioural economics. You have to be smart at letting yourself know that 'this' image is the one that means do a check in (you might have your list written down somewhere and in your pocket/on the desk/next to the console).

Once you have got the hang of this you might change your image/icon, or the order in which you do the check in, because there's nothing like stale or irrelevant content to make you quickly skip or ignore something (think how many adverts you skip past on YouTube for this reason). Brains love novelty (Siegel, 2016) so keep it as exciting as you can with this topic.

Another analogy or way to play with this here is the diet of 'going to the gym' and why people who go to do workouts often mix up their routines for this reason. It takes time to see change, and motivation is key. You may need to set yourself reminders about how you are doing, and go easy on the fails. Reps more than sets here to start.

When you can satisfy the #no-no and #yes-go you will find that you are now moving into the territory of 'intentional' behaviours. This can feel more like *you are in control* and perhaps you will notice the kinds of things you seek out online, engage with, scroll past, hover on when in the spaces of social media. In gaming you might find that you have patterns of types of games for certain reasons, particular people you want to play with and more.

TIMING AND TIMES

Most of us have a device routine. We might not have noticed it fully, but we have found pattern that works for our morning, daytime, nighttime, and weekend schedules. You might just be smiling a little because you know this already. So, let's explore timings and behaviours as most of them will be predictable, somewhat. Again, I invite you to an exercise to help you see the patterns. Rather than writing 'I go on my phone after breakfast' I am going to ask you that for one week you 'notice' your behaviours a little more closely, and this next bit is important: it is important to write your noticing patterns using pen(cil) and paper because of how the brain works when you use this method. Typing it up won't get to the gremlins in the machine adequately or fast enough and it is they who need to hear this.

This exercise might take people weeks to implement due to avoidance, shame, not wanting to change anything etc., so when you do it is up to you.

WHAT YOU WILL DO FOR A WEEK

Notice what you did, where you were, and what time it was, when you first noticed the urge to open the phone, laptop, computer, console etc. for the first time on this day of the week. Much like the behaviours of people who still use radios, they will possibly enter the kitchen and turn on the radio for 'company' before switching the kettle on. Just notice this.

We are not judging the behaviours here, but trying to find the pattern. Is this a wake up, head to the toilet and open the phone kind of behaviour, is this a wake up and check certain apps like weather, social media, or banking kind of behaviour, or is this an after I have eaten breakfast behaviour, or a before I leave the house one? Write this down for each day of the week and weekend. And do this during the day, evening, and night time noting what time, location, and anything else you want to, such as thoughts or feelings for each engagement in social media and or gaming where you can. How you design your diary is up to you and there are plenty of food/activity types online that you could print out and write on or you could make your own which may be more impactful.

WHEN YOU DON'T, DO: SELF-COMPASSION

At this stage I want to interject with a tiny reflection for you: you are doing the best you can in the world, and with the tools that you have. Insight can feel overwhelming, shameful, and shocking at times. Go easy on yourself. Especially when I say it's likely that you will have missed behaviours or timings off the sheets and so there may be more of them than you realise. This is why 'screentime hours' can cause many people to argue with their phone for example. Denial of our social media and gaming 'time' is the easier road to travel. This is an awareness building exercise, and it can really suck to see you are beholden to your device or games and previously thought you were in control. This can be a defining moment for you perhaps. If you want to delve deeply into your behaviours and make permanent changes, then you will need to work with a professional.

At this stage it's okay that you are not Miss Marple or Poirot in being able to put all the clues together just yet. And you're not in therapy but taking a quick steps process from a book. It might work for you, and maybe you need to call that professional.

INTERRUPTS, SELF-TALK, CHECK INS AND DAYS WHEN IT DOESN'T WORK

The way in which CBT helps people and is part of this book is by using that framework, starting with the awareness raising and noticing the pattern to interrupt the pattern. This is often completed for some by forming a new behaviour, a modification of the previous behaviour, or as many of my clients say a new 'habit' (notice it's not called an addiction when it moves in the other direction). Sometimes people are given a helpful phrase that they can say to themselves to notice and deflect an old pattern, for example, 'do I really want to eat that slice of cake? I have eaten one today and in order to reach my goal of… X weight, size, then I need to x, y, z instead' (or whatever the goal is). It looks easy on paper doesn't it?

I am suggesting here is if this worked as easily as it was for me to type it out everyone would succeed at dieting, giving up alcohol, or cigarettes.

The fact is many of us fail, fall short, relapse, and end up eating the darn slice(s) of cake. This is why this part here is to *notice that there will be days when you fail to action, notice or do the diary*. Like mindfulness mantras the noticing is also the noticing and then you can make choices about whether you do the thing, or don't do the thing.

INTERNAL SABOTAGE: THE GREMLIN THE TECH COMPANIES FED AND WATERED

Noticing is just that, so the next part of this helpful advice is how the #no-no list and your behaviours are linked. This is what I would work with in therapy with a client. How and when they started to notice they were spending a lot of time doing the game, social media, or whatever it is. It didn't happen overnight and the slow, dripping tap needed fixing at the outset, when you first noticed a leak, but like many people the world over, it didn't feel so bad, until it did. There may not be a rock bottom for you, but an uncomfortableness and a want to stop. There is always some awareness of what we are doing that we don't want to, but we don't always have the tools. What you might be struggling with is the why you are doing something that you don't particularly like, or that hampers your day, or feels like it's wasted time, or is irrelevant, or is frustrating that 'I did it again!'.

STOPPING A NEED, STOPPING A DISLIKE

The *why someone does this* (for example, spends too much time on…) is twofold; exploitation of a need (of yours) by big tech and you being a human with needs. So really it's the competition between who can meet the need first (or with most appeal). So to untangle this mess it's fairly easy in terms of sabotaging the big tech companies because it's about removing those things that keep you on the device, app, or game for example and these tips and tricks can easily be found by the gurus on the net. For example, telling you to turn the background colours to black and white, to remove notifications from the app or home screen, to install time blockers, to use screentime, downtime and lots of other apps designed to limit your time to moving your social media apps to the last screen on your device and to put a kitchen timer next to the console for the gaming time. These are all great helpful tips and I have linked to some sites in the book to give you some 'digital distraction and avoidance' techniques. Moreover, these distraction techniques are often about reducing the attention that you give to things such as notifications, polarised debates, images, and videos recommended to you. This is the attention economy battle that tech win almost every time.

However, if it was this easy, that is, turning notifications or colours off, then we would all be a little less dependent on these apps and platforms. Seeing as this is not the case this is clearly not the solution but it's a good start and one I recommend in practice.

ATTENTION TO YOUR SELF

The other side of the coin will require you to go into the bushes and fight your own Darth Vader, who turns out to be you, yourself no less! (What a fab scene from Star Wars to illustrate the battles we have with ourselves). Grab your lightsabre and do! (Or do not, but remember there is no try according to the little green guy, Yoda).

Let's start by considering who you might be and what vulnerabilities you may have that those big tech companies are exploiting. Thinking about this you might wonder what kind of question I am asking here; 'how I do know what all my vulnerabilities are?' Perhaps I could name my personality type, I could even take a test online to find out, and that might not be a bad thing. Vulnerabilities though, well that's a different matter.

ACEs THAT ARE FAR FROM 'ACE'

There is a piece of research conducted in the late 1990s that highlighted that many of the adults who were attending a medical facility had experiences in their childhood, classified for a piece of research as being called *adverse childhood* experiences (Felitti et al., 1998). These adversities tended to have one of two outcomes, whereby if you had a person in your life who could support you, who you could turn to and who you could talk to, often the adversity wouldn't have a long-lasting impact versus not having 'a person'. However, this is not to say that just having one person would mean you're not affected by an adverse experience, but certainly being able to reach out to, to talk to, and to get support from *one* other person can often be an incredibly important part of being able to manage (cope). We need others to survive, and here you can see we need others to have good mental health, wellbeing, and well-doing.

Sadly, what the ACE study has shown us is that many children do not have a person to lean on, to talk to, and to gain support from, and suffer from the consequences of the adversity alone and perhaps for a very long time. Now why am I mentioning the ACE study here? Well, it's what we call a starter for ten in the space of understanding what happens to us as children and how we might behave as adults in the real world, and online. The research isn't as robust and plentiful around aces and online behaviour, and this is why I do what I do by writing about and teaching this.

What I can say to you as you read this is those experiences as a child tend to form what we try to resolve, often in our adult life. What we seek is what we were missing. And that might require you to do a deep dive into the difficulties you faced in your childhood. This may be the point in the book where you seek the help of a professional to work with as you do these exercises and think about what is being exploited in you by big tech companies. You may have lots of feelings associated with both aspects.

Most of the advice that exists in books like this, or online, aims to help you make peripheral and superficial changes to your daily behaviours to combat what you might read online as addictive social media or gaming behaviours. What I can't do in this book is what I can do in the therapy room and so what I say here is a superficial as a meme. To understand yourself you really do need to work with a professional who can link innate drives, early childhood experiences and online or gaming activities together. Hopefully they read books like this!

The best I can do in a book is to provide the framework of *noticing*, I cannot explore the deep why with you via a book nor should I or any other author do that. This is why we did the exercise on noticing and behaviours during the day the week and particularly around timing: it gives you the first insight and awareness. The following paragraphs can help you understand a little more but they are only scratching the surface.

Looking at your own needs, what you might call your desires, and what you really want from people, and looking at how these areas overlap into those deep feelings that we brushed past earlier in the chapter, you might be identifying why you are seeking something online through social media and gaming. This may now be surrounded by feelings of shame, deficit, despair, sadness, and loneliness. These are honest, raw, and true feelings and you may never have linked the way in which you grew up to the online space and what you 'do' there before now. You might want to take some time to yourself to process this.

BUILDING A NEW HABIT AND CHAPTER ON SOCIAL MEDIA AND GAMING USE

In the next chapters I look at some positive steps we can make both away from and with technology to provide those positive moments and behaviours. Scaffolding is often how we hold up a building whilst it's being created, removing it when it can stand alone. Support structures form part of a well-designed building. Using that metaphor what goes inside the building is individual as are you, but the structure can be quite generalised.

THE BUILDING ITSELF WILL PERHAPS NEED A BLUEPRINT: FOUNDATION FIRST

It is said willpower is a finite resource, and this usually ebbs at the end of the day (Clear, 2018), and so my suggestion is to use social media and gaming before lunch to ensure that you can use your willpower like a superhero because as the end of the day makes its way towards you, your willpower is lower. Especially after you've had an arduous day's work. Yep, that's a croc and it isn't going to work at all! So, what are the foundational aspects to managing your time with the content?

Those exercises around noticing, timing, needs, early childhood experiences all sync together to produce a recipe for being in those spaces, perhaps longer than you anticipated. And so intentional use can be your lifeline here, only insofar as 'sticking to your plan' and this might mean that you set yourself a time limit or utilise other apps and technology to limit your time. Or you create an evening routine in the same way that new parents create one for the infant in their lives, which can take a small amount of time getting used to, and even in the case of a new infant it radically changes what used to be into what is now.

EVENING ROUTINES

One of the helpful things for maintaining a healthy brain is sleep (Walker, 2018). You probably didn't need to be told that, and you probably have said somewhere along the line that you need to sort your sleep schedule out, because many people don't have good sleep hygiene or say they don't. So how can you create the best environment for a good night's sleep? Simplicity is always key and one of the best ways in which you can create a routine or regime around sleep is to compare it with what a baby requires, and what it feels like to go to bed rested. The aspect I cannot help you with here is most certainly your rumination and anxieties, some of which might be exacerbated by your social media and gaming interactions. But I can certainly give some hints that you can utilise in your life that may start to change the way in which you approach you sleep routine.

DARKNESS

This is going to depend on where you live and the kinds of daylight saving, and seasonal changes that you are surrounded by. But it doesn't take a scientist to work out we sleep best when it's dark and when we're not too hot, hence why lots of hotels have air conditioning. The first thing to acknowledge in your environmental space is what kind of lighting you have for an evening, and can you invest in ways to reduce the brightness of the surrounding light via dimmer switches, coloured bulbs, or candles if you so wish. What is known about sleep hygiene is that light is an indicator to our circadian rhythm and reducing this in an evening can help our brain 'settle for the night' (Panda, 2018).

If you know that bright lights can stimulate your level of wakefulness, then perhaps you can change the screen brightness on your device or monitor or television after sunset. You can also engage colour filters and software can be purchased to change the level of lux (brightness) on your screen and to reduce glare (and the *deadly* blue light).

Perhaps your evening routine can include the use of methods, protocols, or habits such as gentle exercise (relaxation) so that you don't over stimulate your nervous system, and learning how to control your nervous system really is a game changer for sleep. Early childhood experiences can influence your nervous system, so gaining mastery in this is certainly the most recommended benefit for your sleep and your health. You might want to engage in mindful breathing or meditation, and activities such as Yoga Nidra (now commonly called non sleep deep rest), and a warm bath (or sauna) can also give a number of other benefits (mostly this engages the temperature change required for sleep).

ALARM CLOCK OR ALARMING?

Many people I speak to, which includes children, use their device as an alarm clock keeping it in the bedroom for this reason. I would suggest that like a baby who wants to be close to the mother having your device within reach enables you to feel safe in more ways than one, for example should there be an emergency your handy is handy. If you choose to keep your device in the bedroom then utilising the do not disturb function, removing all forms of vibrational notifications, and light activated notifications can be very helpful in allowing restful sleep. This still allows you to use your device as an alarm clock (without your sleep being disturbed during the night).

6

HOW CAN I HELP CHANGE MY CHILD'S HABITS?

DO, PLAY, GO OUTSIDE!

Do your homework, do your jobs or chores, get off the sofa, go out to play! I don't get it. Why won't they do something else? They're even watching someone else play a game not doing it themselves, what's that all about?

I think that sums up what parents say to me most often in my clinic, in training, and in nearly all the conversations I have with them (including friends and family). They say (or shout) at their children to 'do more in the real world', and usually follow this up with 'back in my day', and sometimes I hear; 'we're the first generation to know before and after the internet, kids these days…'

And so almost each parent, carer, or guardian is stuck. Most of my work with parents is done in the therapy space and educating practitioners. Those practitioners are quite often parents too and invariably as I teach, the parent inside the professional emerges as the dominant 'listener' in the room. I tend to hear panic, concern, and confusion in the adults as they want to protect their children.

So, let's go back to the research that we discussed in the earlier chapters. When it comes to parenting a child who is 'using' technology there is a slight disconnect by and with the adults in the understanding of why a child is doing what they're doing (for more

DOI: 10.4324/9781032617251-7

information on this do check out my other books where I explain this in more detail, Knibbs, 2022, 2023a, 2023b). Some of the research discussed in the earlier chapters looks at issues of children being sedentary and of course what we've all been taught about sitting is 'it's the new smoking'. We've probably grown up with a narrative around what it is to be lazy and how it is scorned (by parents, teachers, and society). As you read that word lazy you might have conjured up an image of somebody committing one of the seven deadly sins of sloth, or a stereotypical 'couch potato' as this is the most common language around laziness.

Adverts and the communication by the medical and health industries tells us we need to exercise 150 minutes per week (that's vigorous zone 2 to zone 3 exercise, https://www.nhs.uk/live-well/exercise/exercise-guidelines/physical-activity-guidelines-for-adults-aged-19-to-64/), which is beneficial for us, however, we are fully aware that often *we* don't achieve that as the adults, so we can project towards the children that they need to do more, move, and move more!

VALUE… LESS?

Some of the other things that parents tell me in the therapy room is that their children, when using social media or gaming, are not using the cognitive part of their brain, as it's *just* gaming or browsing on social media for example (having never explored what the child is doing or what they interact with for more than five minutes). Parents and carers tell me they *just know* that the child is doing something that is *valueless*. The question I ask here of parents is: how would you know that there is no value to what they are engaging with (online or through gaming) until you could effectively do some sort of test or exam about that engagement, to ascertain whether it had value or not? For example, a child might be watching a YouTube video, a tutorial no less, in order that they can understand how to do something practical that otherwise they might not be able to do, because they didn't understand it in the classroom. The fact an influencer might explain something in a slightly different way, with a show and tell process, might just be the value that that child takes from this. We call that learning. A great example here is taken from several of my clients in therapy under the age of 11 who have done exactly this (with me or at home). A child who watches a Minecraft streamer engaging in the creation of a portal into the *end or nether world*. A five-year-old watching this tutorial can now copy, remember, and replicate this. This gives them some information that they can share with their siblings, parents, or peers in the classroom, which aids in social communication and a shared connection. The value of watching the video about gaming can give a child several skills in several domains. Not useless but useful.

A further example is a child on social media, who on the outside looks like she's browsing Facebook. For this example, let's pretend Millie wants to understand the complexities behind black holes because these sounded exciting in science. She searched YouTube when she got home, found some information about the scientist explaining the concept of black holes. She noticed their name, and decided to see if they also had a Facebook page or group that she could join. Millie joined a Facebook group where the community of people within that group discussed some of the science behind black holes and how a few years ago a female scientist was revered for putting together the first photograph of a black hole. Millie told me in therapy that she also wanted to become a scientist, or astronaut, or astrophysicist. She wanted to talk to me about black holes and how exciting they were now that she had more knowledge than had been taught in the classroom. This was now encouraging her to study physics and that she would take this option through her GCSEs and would likely make further education choices around this career. Millie also spent several hours listening to podcasts, buying books, and watching discussions online. The value Millie found in using social media supported her interest and career choice. This is like the 20th-century assembly talk she might have received from an astronaut, where she then visited a library to read around astrophysics (if anyone still uses a library like this).

But beware the 'all content is good content' thinking, as this process is the same process that takes place when watching an influencer who might suggest (to children) to engage in something that might not be healthy.

The value is in the content, and this is what we need to be discussing with children through conversations rather than just looking at the outward behaviour, or a child sitting looking into a device without fully understanding '*what* are they are doing in there'.

WATCH WHAT THEY WATCH WITH THEM

The first piece of advice in this chapter around helping the adult to help the child is to think about what the child is doing, what content they engage with, why that might be helpful, or truthful or what we call malinformation, misinformation, disinformation (Knibbs, 2023b), or downright lies. Now what this means in actuality for the adult is that they will have to engage in conversations that they might have no interest in whatsoever (constant discussions about Obsidian blocks, farming or crafting in Minecraft might sound boring, boring, boring). Perhaps it is a topic you don't understand yourself, for example black hole physics, statistics, or golf. Perhaps parents feel they don't have the time to explore what a child is interested in, or who (influencer, celebrity, or streamer) a child is interested in. To do this really does mean you as the adult would have to look at the same content that your child is looking at. I hear a few sighs at this prospect. Over the years PewDiePie, KSI and Mr Beast (https://www.independent.co.uk/life-style/top-digital-influencers-instagram-youtube-pewdiepie-kdi-saffron-barker-a9096486.html) have all taught me something about why children watch them, and each influencer has literally driven me to mind-numbing moments for which I will never get my time back.

But *I needed to watch with the children to understand their reasons for watching.*

Now, I get that parents and adults need to work, and in their own time want to use social media or gaming for their own pleasure. To consider that you might now have to start engaging with the same content as your children means your 24-hour day just increased by another six hours. It sounds an impossibility! And yet, this is not so if we think about quality time *with* our children. I'm suggesting here the time you spend with your child must include sharing some of their online and gaming activities. Not all of it, all the time of course, as no one has that amount of time! This can help you understand the engagement time needed to 'follow' and keep up to date with the popular things (games, conversations, or trends), that their friends are often interested in too.

SO HOW DO WE MANAGE THIS?

Parenting can be a very difficult job at times, and there's only so many times you can read the Gruffalo (Donaldson, 2016) before you know it off by heart. Nursery rhymes that are possibly stuck at the back of your head might just be memories of when you had time to sit with your little one and sing the songs. Once children move into education, parents offload some of their duty to those who teach. Parents pass on that baton so that they can work and earn an income, so their child can have a device, which let's face it can be a (suitable?) babysitter when we have no time. Acknowledging that we have (in the past) or do leave our children in front of devices in order that we can cook dinner, clean the dog, wash the car, or do the zoom meetings means that they engage in social spaces with other people that might meet their needs and frees up a little of our time. We are not monsters, but busy adults.

To know that sometimes we are massively busy, at times we don't really care, we are bored or fed up with what our children talk about is something that I don't see discussed in the space of e-safety. It's like the rule is you don't ever leave your child unsupervised. It's unmanageable, impossible, untenable, and blames you the parents or carers for the time you do allow unsupervised access. We must have a space that gives us permission to be fed up with, and uninterested in our children or what they are doing sometimes, because: fact. I do see so often the eye rolls from the adults when technology is mentioned, or specific games or the dramas taking place for example on WhatsApp. We have so much going on in our own heads like all the things we need to do or have responsibility for as adults that sometimes we really don't want to listen.

> *We must have a more compassionate approach to parenting in the digital age; what I see is the narrative of; you need to be 'expert psychologist, technologist, scientist, educator, therapist and Inspector Gadget, helicopter spyware parent' and no excuses!*

THE 'IT'S YOUR FAULT' NARRATIVE

I wonder how it feels to know you're not alone in thinking that social media companies, all the drama online, and even digital jargon is getting in the way of what used to be a very lovely relationship with you and your tiny person who didn't chat back, or scream at you when you ask them to sit down for their dinner (actually I take that back: some toddlers do this). Reminiscing about a time when you could understand your children's wants and needs. Perhaps what technology has really done is create a distance, a divide between you and your child. The most difficult aspect of that is when parents say, 'I gave them the darn device! It's my fault'. This can leave adults feeling like they caused the problem or are at fault. Angered by this they may blame the technology companies or their children.

There is an element of truth to the technology companies' responsibility here as *they exploit children's needs to keep them on the platform*, in the same way they manipulate and exploit you (as discussed in the earlier chapters). It is easier to exploit children though because they do not have the adult thinking brain. Many parents in today's world are very stuck with the juxtaposition of giving technology to their child, delaying it, and many not knowing that the media companies would exploit their children in this way. Sadly, parents and carers are the ones left with the behavioural outcomes seen every day in homes.

So here are some things you can do and have a little control with.

MOVE!

There is quite the push to get and keep children engaged in physical activity, usually within education settings. However, one of the difficulties that I am beginning to see with the children who come into my therapy office is that the amount of movement they can engage in within school and extracurricular activities is being limited by the need to perform academically. Some primary schools within the United Kingdom are reducing the amount of play sessions that take place during the day, and certainly by the age of ten the focus is on passing tests called SATS (https://www.gov.uk/national-curriculum/key-stage-1-and-2). This means children are sitting for longer in a classroom and that requires the nervous system to hold in a whole heap of energy that children of this age have. So, no it's not all technology, gaming and social media's fault! This is our education system and it's creating a sedentary society before the age of 11, which extends to 16 and beyond (as education is in some cases mandatory to 18), before heading off to university. Education has a part to play here, but don't let me distract you with this knowledge, blame the tech!

JIGGLE, WIGGLE, AND TWITCH (NOT THE PLATFORM): NERVOUS SYSTEMS AND THEIR NEED TO EXPRESS ENERGY!

Imagine winding a spring tighter and tighter during the day, and only releasing it when the home time bell rings. In the classroom education takes place relatively slowly in comparison to a fast-paced game. And so, if you *have energy that you've been collecting* (a way to think about this energy process), all day long like a solar battery, you're likely going to want to expend that energy. Quite often this is why children can be the screaming, shouty, excitable 'Duracell bunny' gamer. Or indeed they can be the haphazard wizard, multi-platform, social media 'bunny app hopper'. You might even notice when children are sitting with devices that their nervous systems are expending that energy by the jiggles in their legs, shoulder movements, neck clicking and thumbs that move at lightning speed. They need to get rid of the compressed energy, and the children with attentional difficulties seem to have more of this energy.

A great resource is the idea of movement 'snacks' which are tiny moments throughout the day where one to two minutes of exercise takes place, but you can make it fun by opting to move like an animal (Edwards, 2021).

MACCY D's, KFC, AND DOUGHNUTS

In physical exercise and nutrition disciplines there is a conversation about something called NEAT (Baker & Norton, 2019). This is a form of energy expenditure that takes place in all of us, but is particularly high in some children and is that constant tiny set of movements. NEAT can result in calorie expenditure and is usually assessed as part of a person's daily count. One of the worries that many parents have is that if a child is not engaging in a high energy exercise such as running, skipping, football, netball, or rounders (some of these are UK based games that children play in school) or other forms of childhood games that *we played* such as tag, tig (depending on which part of the UK you're from), tree climbing and apple scrumping, hide and seek or even what time is it Mr Wolf, then we are equating the lack of outdoor movement in a child once they arrive home as being completely different '*to when we were young*'.

Now I'm not saying that being on games or social media in a sedentary position for extended periods is great, and certainly at times when I was writing this book I did a lot of that myself. What seems to be getting confused about is what is the expected time for exercise that a child should engage in, where do they engage in this exercise, how long do they engage in exercise for, and what is the recommended amount for your child given a large number of factors which cannot always be measured (genetic variations, bone density, ability if there is a disability, and an accurate count on calorie intake versus energy expenditure).

It seems the issue may be more to do with calorie intake whilst snacking (Heitman et al., 2023), gaming, or playing on devices that causes much of the obesity and weight issues. Snacks that the children of the 1970s or 1980s ate were not as calorie dense, freely available, or promoted as part of the experience. See my other books for the health and harms chapter (Knibbs, 2023b).

> *Snacks and high sedentary lifestyles seem to be the health harm, not the social media-ing or gaming alone.*

MOTIVATION: WHERE IS THE Wii AND KINECT?

The NHS in the United Kingdom suggests that children should be taking part in exercise at school and suggests after school activities as being helpful (https://www.nhs.uk/live-well/exercise/exercise-guidelines/physical-activity-guidelines-children-and-young-people/). A question I have here is, if a child has a diagnosis of autism and struggles with posture, coordination, and social communication, how easy is it for a parent to get that child to engage in a large group after school activity? And, how easy is it for that child to go home, pick up a controller, sign into their gaming console and engage with other children there where they feel somewhat in control?

When we think of movement, and gaming, one of the experiences that I like to discuss with the adults I'm working with is remembering how the Nintendo Wii brought families together to engage in physical activities and gaming. Kinect from Xbox also attempted to create this space. But isn't it interesting how many families did not keep up this exercise regime through gaming and how 'defunct' Wii and Kinect are now? Why haven't these 'at home, fun experiences' remained? Why haven't the adults kept this aspect of healthy behaviour in their home, why do exergames trail off and where is the motivation from adults here?

EXERGAMES AND ENERGY

Now we are moving into the immersive worlds of virtual reality and exercise, called exergames, I wonder if the argument about movement is going to subside when we see an uptake in more games that require high energy, for example, a very popular game at the time of writing for many of the children I work with is gorilla tag. Sweaty children, sweaty headsets, and lots of movement. Not a typical exercise game and it is popular with so many children. Fantastic! I hope that there are many headsets bought towards the end of 2023 to increase this type of movement in children.

FOOD CUPBOARD AND FRIDGE CHOICES

What is known about food and mood in the spaces of nutritional health and well-being is a common discussion and is much deeper than I can write about here in depth. I am introducing you to the idea that what you consume can indeed impact how you feel (Naidoo, 2020). But it is more important that some of those processed food groups are consumed quite often whilst children are engaged in social media or gaming activities as discussed above (https://newzoo.com/resources/blog/gamer-food-and-drink-consumption-consumer-brands-consumer-insights). Whilst this is not entirely a section on 'getting your child off' devices, games, or tech, it is a way to support their health long term. I feel this is important in this book as this is about the holistic approach to managing what we do in a world of tech.

One thing you can do as an adult is decide on the kinds of food that make it from the supermarket shelf to your cupboards and your fridge. I'm aware the market of quick and easy isn't a recent invention (the microwave appeared decades ago). So many of us have become accustomed to quick food solutions for our family when we are busy, working late, or have lots of after school clubs to attend. It's like a catch 22 situation where keeping our children in spaces that enable them to be doing exercise can result in eating habits that become less than healthy overall. Unless you have a full-time chef at home, many of us choose to take the small packages off the shelf, the 'ding dinners' or we head to the fast food emporium. It's ubiquitous easy reach ultra-processed and junk food heaven.

Non-processed foods are those you will find underground overground (and womble-ing free), They grow freely, and generally are found in the fresh or frozen aisles in a supermarket, plain on their own and require cooking for more than a nine-minute 'ding dinner' (microwave). These are meats, fruit, nuts, grains, spices, and vegetables.

I wonder what your child would say if you only kept fruit, nuts, and vegetables for snacks? I'm almost imagining your face and the thought process of 'but what about the treats Cath?' And therein lies the way that most of us think about food in the current climate of needing *something for being good*. I wonder what your relationship with food and treats are (healthy versus unhealthy)? Many spaces online (cinema and TV too) advertise products dressed up as healthy alternatives. How are you to know whether they are or not healthy unless you have a degree in nutrition? Our children watch what we eat, what is advertised to them, and what they engage with online. Again, the health chapter in my other book is helpful here (Knibbs, 2023b). What we can do is model the model and have nutritious foods in our homes, often not calorie dense and that might need a little imagination to create a great looking dish or snack. Your future self will thank you, and so will your child when they do not have health issues related to overconsumption of ultra-processed, calorie dense, nutritionally deficient foods.

THEY ONLY EAT FLAT-BROWN-BEIGE-BORING, WHAT CAN I DO?

I am aware that many of the children I work with in my therapy practise that have a diagnosis of autism quite often struggle with the texture, smell, and complexities of foods that might require an adult to spend 30 to 60 minutes in a kitchen preparing. Many children with sensory difficulties have an aversion to specific foods or groups (Çekici & Sanlier, 2017). Often when we look at a cohort of children with this diagnosis, who reportedly and anecdotally spend a large amount of their time online (whether that be gaming or using social media), it can be extremely difficult to introduce the food groups that I've talked about above.

For example, carrot sticks are certainly not a staple favourite of many of the children I work with, including those with a diagnosis of autism, and their preference tends to be in the space of flat shelf cooker foods such as waffles, potato smiles, chicken nuggets, chips, or pizza. Or they tend to enjoy junk fast foods such as McDonalds. They tend not to eat salad, stew, or other homemade dinners with sauces etc. (for many reasons not covered in this book). Many of the parents that I work with in this cohort opt for an easy route, without understanding the long term health implications of these food groups, where there is a lack of diversity and nutrition.

My thinking is (backed up by my studies in nutrition), many of these children are malnourished in the form of micronutrients and this can exacerbate behavioural presentations such as tics, movement jiggles, and regulatory capacities of self-soothing mechanisms. Mood and food are tied together harmoniously, or not, depending on what we feed it (our guts) (Palmer, 2023).

MODUS OPERANDI

We live in a complex world, and when we think about helping children who are online both gaming and in social media, we need to think about their modus operandi for being in that space. To have those discussions about what they are doing, why, who with, what for, how long, and how this can interact with their wants and needs around the real-world practicalities of exercise, community, and nutrition. We need to check in with our why, our modus operandi too, and what we want from our children in this space. Do we provide a boundaried, respectable, and emotionally resonant household? Or do we have a screen time contract that is non-negotiable because some guru on the internet showed us how to create a legal style document with which to enforce device time in the house?

WHAT DO I MEAN BY THIS?

Most importantly, being able to help our child involves us being grounded, emotionally available, and present. We are not the rule makers that never break, or breakers that never make. Parenting around tech can be ever-changing, depending on ages and stages and who is in their life (friends, hobbies, relatives, etc.). As I said, one of the handiest hints that I've seen online for several years now is for parents to have a social media contract, gaming calendar, or whatever you want to call it, which involves a limited amount of time that you allow your child to use the device for gaming or social media and what your expectations are around dinner, exercise, and most importantly bedtime (https://digitalwellnesslab.org/guides/parents-guide-to-creating-shared-media-use-agreements/). And, what the consequences might be if the contract is broken. Sadly, I see children bashed with this, rather than supported, so let's take a look at what research has shown to be a connected way to parent. This means that we give and gain respect, the ability to converse, trust, and be trusted. And if you want to out manoeuvre the perpetrators of crimes against children in those online spaces you will need to create those channels of trust and conversations.

CPR! THREE ELEMENTS TO CONNECTED PARENTING AND HOUSEHOLD HARMONY

When I work with parents one of the things we often discuss in the sessions are parenting styles which can be of several types; we are attempting to avoid overly liberal or authoritarian. One of the more important aspects of parenting which can impact attachment styles, is how consistent a parent might be (Bowlby, 1997). I help my parents to understand CPR for household harmony. OK I might have lied about the *always harmony* aspect as you'll see in just a moment as children don't always like rules and want to butt up against them, and that can be far from harmonious.

Consistency

C in CPR means to be *consistent*; this doesn't mean ruling with an iron fist it means having a *process within you* by which you parent. That will include your values, ethics, compassion, empathy, and most of all emotional regulation of yourself. Not always easy to do, easy to write about of course, and can be obvious when a third person helps you interpret what's going on in the moment. As of this moment in time we don't have AI bots in our houses helping us demystify and understand what it is that our child is trying to communicate to us, so this is where the consistency responsibility lands on us in terms of our approach to our child.

Now what does this really mean? Consistency sounds like how we might observe the texture of a smoothie or cake mixture and I'm sure if you've ever made either of these you know consistency has a little bit of leeway and so will we in this parenting (profession). We're not looking for rules about technology that are completely unbendable, neither are we looking for rules that are so lax that nobody can understand them or when they are applied. Our consistency is a way of looking at our parenting in the same way a therapist or a school might look at a behaviour through a trauma informed lens (https://www.traumainformedschools.co.uk/home/what-is-a-trauma-informed-school). And what this means in practicality is each parent's lens is individual here.

The theory behind why we do what we do, and when we do it, and what for, is the mainstay of how we are consistent. For example, you ask your child to come off a game because you have relatives over, and it is now dinner time. How you implement the request to end the game and sit at the table for dinner will be in the same vein as when it's Friday night, you're really tired from a hard week at work, and your child is 'whiny, needy, using that voice, argumentative or screaming'. We approach the situations with the same level of understanding, patience, and language (tone, loudness etc) of ourselves and our child and we are child centred not 'me' centred.

Being child centred does not mean that we allow the child to rule the roost, nor does it mean we are soft, or give in easily. It does mean we take the perspective of the child in our thinking and how we observe what the child is doing today and why etc. Yes, you must be on your toes and each interaction with a child is different (even compared to ten minutes ago) and I'm sure you've noticed at some point that what they liked last week is not the same as this week. Quite often parents will say in the therapy room that children are fickle and have fads and they are confused by this. Perhaps they just have a more varied way of seeing the world because they are still discovering who they are. They do not have the capacity that we do as adults to be consistent, and therefore that process lies with us.

A quick example of consistency towards a child who; 'won't come off their device' is to remind the child of the agreement you have, and the choice they have, and what consequences might follow should their choice break your agreement. Utilising parenting techniques that are supportive such as attachment parenting, two-choice choices (limiting the options), and natural consequences and being consistent in choosing to parent like this is the first part of the three aspects in CPR.

Persistence

The P is for persistence. This is not *nagging* your child but holding firm with your consistency and persisting in a way that I call broken record parenting. For example, when explaining to a child that our session is ending some children may engage in delay tactics whereby they get a new toy out, and notice a new thing, which really isn't new, but in this moment, it really really is! One of the ways that I would engage in consistency and persistence is to explain to the child that our session must end as it did last week, and I might use reflections on how frustrating or sad this might be, and yet the persistence is I reflect the session *is still* ending. This technique acknowledges the child's feelings, and quite often I will also reflect that their behaviour tells me they still want to be in the room and I can see that and understand that, and the persistence of my consistency is to remain firm *but our time has ended for today*, and I will often remind the child that we have another session next time and that today's ending is not forever. But *for today we must come to an end*.

Children require and need boundaries to feel safe. There have been experiments that have looked at children in a playground, where around the perimeter there was no fence, versus when a fence is or was installed. Where the children congregated or move to when the fence was installed increased to the perimeters (https://www.asla.org/awards/2006/studentawards/282.html). This experiment shows us that when there are boundaries children move more freely. Many of these boundaries are well established in education settings, such as time to start and time to finish both the school day and lessons. Whilst there might be some behaviours around attending school or lessons or leaving them, most children feel the safety of these timings because they are predictable. When it comes to the C and the P in CPR the first two are the boundaries that enable children to understand where their freedom and challenge limits are. And that brings us to the R.

Resistance

The R in CPR is for resistance. To what you might ask? Well, that's the boundary pushing that will inevitably happen, and this is where the harmony I mentioned may not be in full force! When boundaries are put in place, as in the end of the session example I gave earlier, then children will push or pull those boundaries to see how strong your consistency and persistence really, truly are. The resistance here applies to the way in which children will plead, beg, and recruit all other strategies they have, that could potentially create a break in your boundaries. If this happens it can leave them feeling unsafe and not knowing how predictable their world will be. Your resistance to their techniques is what helps them feel safer in the long term. And I know how tortuous this time can feel when the pleading and crying turns to anger, and anger leads to hate. Which apparently leads to the dark side. Tough you must be!

As a quick reflection here: one of the consistent, persistent, and resistant limitations that gaming offers children are boundaries, in many different ways such as numbers of lives, areas on the gaming map where they can navigate, ways in which they can advance and or point scoring rules by giving detailed instructions. This is why children are so miffed when other players *cheat or hack* around those rules and boundaries that the game offers. Predictability is how we feel safe (Siegel, 2010) even when we think about games or social media, and this is why it's easy for us to be provoked by people who don't play by the rules.

I would also like to reflect here: one of the reasons I love working with children is because of their tendency for out of the box thinking around pushing those boundaries to see how my CPR meets their needs, but the most impressive thing is the genius behind the adaptability, creativity, and resourcefulness of ways in which they can think outside the box to *take you out like a boss* in a game. This creativity is so often hampered by the lack of power they have in the world (and Sir Ken Robinson (2007) talked about how this is missing in the education systems on his TED talk). When I hear of a way in which a child has pushed those boundaries, I am impressed at their smarts, their thinking, planning, and reasoning behind such behaviour which is mostly driven by needs and not manipulation. Children are incredible and I marvel at them in this way.

BEDTIME AND BRAIN DEVELOPMENT

Now to keep that thinking brain healthy and developing for a life without cognitive issues (before old age), the paradigm of sleep is important (Walker, 2018). One of the things I spend a lot of time talking to my child clients (nine to 25 years of age) about is their brain health. This is not taught nearly enough in schools, and many parents are not aware either of things that can help and hinder everyday brain functioning, optimal performance, and brain health. And so this part of the chapter is going to refer to sleep and then I will tie in much of what we've talked about so far. You can then talk to your child with information that they might find fascinating (or not).

Pre-birth babies are isolated from the day and night cycle, what is called the circadian rhythm, by the very fact they are within the womb.

If we consider new-born babies beginning their circadian rhythm in a world where they have never seen or been around day or night-time, in varying seasons, you can begin to understand why it's so difficult for them to adapt to our adult world.You might have noticed babies sleep a lot, and what science shows us is that brain development (and good health) requires sleep which is made-up of cycles throughout the night. It is only in one of these cycles that certain elements of brain health processes take place, whereas others promote learning and memory (Walker, 2018). Consider how much you sleep when you are poorly to heal from whatever virus or bacteria that is hampering your body at the time.

Before and during adolescence

Most (not all), younger children up to approximately age eight or nine will have a particular sleeping pattern (this may look historically different from children born pre-1990). This section is probably going to be the most important for children who are heading into adolescence, and puberty (which is said to be starting earlier for many children around the world, Farello et al., 2019). Adolescence is where brain development is going through its own process, alongside puberty (Siegel, 2014), alongside all the issues around the use of devices or gaming, late at night, through the night, or toward bedtime. In the 21st century this may be a starkly different sleeping pattern compared to the 20th century. More research here please!

Adolescents are said to require anywhere between nine and 13 hours sleep per night (Siegel, 2014) and I'm sure that's not happening for many (regardless of the tech 'battles'). The requirement for this amount of sleep is because the brain is going through the same kinds of processes that occurred in infancy. The architecture and connections in the brain are being built, in this case to become an adult brain, and that requires a lot of energy a lot of rest and a lot of cycles of sleep (slow wave sleep, commonly called deep sleep). Adolescents may need more cycles of slow wave sleep compared to an older adult and so it will be helpful if I explain how these cycles work very briefly. Do read the books that I've recommended at the back of this book regarding this topic.

Sleep!

Sleep is, simply put, made-up of cycles of four different types: light, Slow Wave Sleep (SWS), Rapid Eye Movement (REM), and awake (moving about for example and generally following deeper stages). SWS and REM add together to make what is called 'restorative sleep' (https://www.whoop.com/us/en/; https://ouraring.com/).

The REM stage allows for processes to occur within the brain around memory consolidation and learning (Walker, 2018). This is even appearing in an advert for nappies (diapers) where a baby is shown to be mimicking movements that they did during the day. In the SWS cycle, there are several important neurotransmitters and processes taking place to help the brain rid itself of the accumulated gunk (the byproducts of working hard!). In science terms this is the glymphatic system that is pushing out the excess toxins, metabolites, and other waste compounds from the day's activities (Walker, 2018). If this clearing out process does not take place it can impact on the following day. For example, you might feel groggy, have brain fog, or forgetful.

I've noticed if I tell young people about these processes they are usually quite surprised and often want to take care of their brain health because they don't want to be 'dumb, forgetful or slow' (their words). This gives us a space to talk about how they can implement changes around bedtime, sleep, and waking that don't always involve technology; however in the next chapter I will be discussing how technology can be a positive help in this area.

Light! Blue, or otherwise

The debate about blue light has been very interesting: one wavelength has been demonised for keeping people awake at night time, blue! The way in which the eyes work is extremely impressive, yet

I have never found in any of the optical theories that I have studied that eyes are able to filter out one wavelength alone. The *hype behind blue light* can be seen with a critical eye (sorry for the pun). It can be about sales of eyeglasses or software that can prevent this form of light entering the eyeball. There is quite a bit of research about the *glare* emitted from a device that includes *all wavelengths* (https://www.hubermanlab.com/newsletter/using-light-for-health). Because the glow of a screen is often perceived as being of a blue colour it has become the demon wavelength and now the health gurus online will tell you this is the frequency of ultraviolet.

To take you back to your primary and high school physics and biology: what you may have learned about light is that it is made-up of many colours, and you might remember spinning a (Newton) disc (of all the colours) to find they blend into a white shade (https://www.stem.org.uk/resources/elibrary/resource/28166/newton-wheel). What we do know about our eyes is that those of us without any macular dysfunction have a lens that allows all spectrum of light through the to the back of the eye where the rods and cones do their job. And it is suggested that it is the *brightness* that is *the lux* of the light emitted from a device or your lamps and lights after sundown that can trigger feelings of alertness and lack of sleepiness. The consequences of this are that a *hormone* called melatonin is not produced in the right quantities, at the right time, to induce sleepiness (https://www.hubermanlab.com/newsletter/using-light-for-health). Devices do emit bright light and it is this that may be causing some of this issue. This is quite a distinct difference from the days of candlelit evenings before the invention of the lightbulb. The sale of what are called blue blocking glasses are not necessarily something to be scoffed at (which I have done as well as using them a number of years ago), because they reduce *the brightness* of the light entering the eye, as would sunglasses. But the evidence for getting better sleep due to using them is still a hung jury.

One technique I introduce to parents is to invest in a dimmer switch wherever possible for all lighting systems throughout the house so that after sundown light levels can be reduced to help with the production of melatonin and to calm the nervous system. Orange and red filters or bulbs can be acquired to create the biological equivalent of a campfire feelings, which is how our biology performs its best for sleep (Walker, 2018).

Conversely, I also suggest to parents and young people that they invest in *free* behaviours that can help set the circadian rhythm (which is the timing of light and hormone regulation systems needed for the functioning of many biological processes not discussed in detail here in this book) which include viewing daytime light (that is, not staring at the sun) early in the morning when the sun has risen, without glasses, not inside the house and not through a window (https://www.hubermanlab.com/newsletter/using-light-for-health). An open door or window will suffice if you live in England where rain is a constant companion. This may seem like a silly intervention, however there is much science behind this free, easily committable, morning routine that can result in a more cohesive body and brain synchronicity. (I write about this in my early books and suggest people listen to the podcasts by Andrew Huberman's (2023), who is an expert in this area). Good luck, you can usually see results in a few days of this behaviour.

Do your chores/homework or lose the device?

I purposefully left this section towards the end, because homework can be a battle for many parents, for a variety of reasons. I find from working with parents and professionals that homework is used as a bargaining tool, a must do or punitive activity. So a quick thought experiment is: I wonder how you would feel after working very hard at work, coming home knowing your favourite television programme is airing in an hour (if anybody still watches television), and that you cannot watch your programme until you have completed your chores, done all of the admin paperwork that relates to your job, prepared and cooked dinner, fed the dog, repaired the cupboards or toilet and washed the car before 'being allowed' to watch your favourite TV show?

For many of the children I work with what they tell me about leaving education and going home is that this is the place where they just want to chill and engage with their friends in online activities. What they tell me relates to all the paragraphs above, they may not or don't have time during the school day to socialise. Some friends are not even in their school or geographic location. I'm sure you remember as a young person what you wanted to do when you got home was 'play out'. Children know that homework is there to help them understand the subjects they are doing at school. Chores help them learn how to be independent. But they just don't want to, or like to, and would rather play out, in this case be online with friends. They often do not understand the concept of discipline and delayed gratification about skills for later life, because the world of the 'influencer' offers an easy way to be successful and earn compared to the skills of a master craftsperson.

Some children will tell me that they should be doing schoolwork in school (which makes logical sense), and not at home because that is their time to be with their friends. We seem to have a double bind when we suggest to children that they develop skills in the domains of socialising, but then hold them to ransom about their homework or chores, when often we haven't had a conversation about other families' timetables to know when their friends are available. Perhaps Billy at number 9 needs to wait for Dad to get home to help with his homework so he can play on the PS until 6pm. Perhaps Laila has to wait until 7pm after caring for her siblings and her Mum who is at home with palliative carers. Ben may not get to play until 9pm after football and swimming, or before he goes out to sports at 6:30pm.

Some children want to actively get the homework out of the way before play and some children like doing their homework. So the chores and homework issue may not even be one for some families at all. I suspect there are many people reading this with children who do not like to do homework or chores and so the device or times on it becomes the power dynamic of threat, pleading, and punishment from the parent to the child.

*Resentment: **** off mum, you don't get it*

Some parents are not attempting to be *mean*, yet this word is uttered by both children and adults as the outcome of the removal of the console, device, or time on the computer/smartphone. Some parents use devices and consoles as punitive tools or weapons (not physical ones I hope). Parents have suggested to me that children are 'wasting their time, ignoring them, kicking off for no reason, horrible when they are pulled off the game, wrong for wanting to do the gaming or social media' etc. When parents remove those devices, often in anger, spite, or punishment the children tell me all trust is gone, and they do not want to engage in a relationship with their parent, because they are mean and 'they don't get me or why this is important'.

Remember the chapter on needs and thinking patterns? It's much easier to be angry with you than feel shame and so this often turns into resentment towards you. Or compliance to be able to have their device etc. Many adults have been educated in this way as children, into being *compliant silent*, it's not a healthy interpersonal and intrapersonal place.

Now I'm not saying here at all that children do not have to do their homework, nor should devices ever be taken away from children, nor am I telling you how to parent. What I do know is that negotiating boundaries, CPR, and in this case getting homework done, is a balancing act, more often on a day-to-day basis with some ups and downs, rather than an easy done deal every day. Utilising a child centred approach, with the focus on what a child is required to do and for what reasons might be a more palatable, harmonious way in which to achieve the outcome. To do this the child has to be involved in that outcome. And what I mean by this is communicating with a child to find out why the resistance and discord around homework exists, and most importantly here discussing consequences of behaviour which include removing access to certain things such as the internet, time on a device or game, and *the why*. This is where a technology contract comes in handy: break the contract and… (you will have already had this conversation when setting it up).

One of the ways in which you can converse with adolescents more successfully is to ask them about their future and what they want to achieve as a career perhaps. Maybe help them think about procrastination now having an impact later, rather than saying 'wasting your time on…'. When having a conversation about what it takes to achieve a career prospect you might find you get answers such as I want to be a streamer, professional gamer, e-sports champion, influencer, and other online activity related professions. The educational requirement for some of these professions certainly doesn't ally with 'must achieve x GCSEs'. So, when as a parent you find yourself saying things like 'you need to pass your Maths or English' you will often find a retort that counteracts this statement, so be aware of this boundary push!

This future career thinking can be quite difficult for younger children and I'm going to suggest thinking on a shorter timeline, weekly or monthly perhaps. Ask what it is a child wants to achieve or buy from a toy shop for example. Homework and chores can be a step rather than an obstacle to achieving that.

'In order to have or do A, *what is it you need to do today/now*, so that you can have that item, profession or achieve A'.

GOAL SETTING AND GOAL GETTING: YOU AND THE CHILDREN

When we have goals, we can look at helpful behaviours to achieve the goal. We can employ consequences rather than punishments for not actioning those behaviours. Children can learn autonomy, agency, and self-control with guidance, but they still need assistance. The psychological language for this is they still need *co-regulation* (sometimes even in their early 20s) (Siegel, 1999/2020). A child centred approach means an understanding that children are not adults (even when they are tall and are nearing their 20s) and that they do not always have the capacity or resilience to fulfil those behaviours that are crucial and critical to achieving the goal they set. This is where parenting can feel more like coaching, and based on their strengths and that we want to support rather than creating the compliant silent through nagging, pushing, and blackmailing.

I suspect those behaviours didn't work for you as a child, so when we consider children's use of technology this form of carrot and stick is often useless, yet it is the most common parenting I hear of.

Good luck in your parenting, remembering all the aspects here may take a while and re-reading this book (and my earlier ones may be of benefit too). It took me a long time, and I still don't always get it right. Emotions in parenting sometimes crop up, paved with many trips and falls. I am the expert at this for sure. One of the most helpful pieces of information I ever received from my training therapy was: there will always be ruptures in our relationships with our children, and the most important thing about this is *the repair is the glue* that keeps us connected.

7

IT ISN'T ALL BAD, IS IT? WHAT ARE THE POSITIVES OF GAMING AND SOCIAL MEDIA?

THERE WAS ONCE AN ADVERT THAT CLAIMED 'INT MILK BRILLIANT!'[1]

And in the same excited tone: *so is tech which includes social media and gaming*. The benefits of the spaces online that we can visit have vastly increased what is possible for finding joy and connection, or what can be achieved by human beings in terms of inventions and progress. This chapter is a full cheer approach to technology and the positives that I have seen, heard, and discussed in therapy, witnessed as a human behaviour technologist, and talk about myself. This is when excited I can often be heard to say, 'my giddy pants!'

Many of the books I write, lectures I give, courses I run, and work I do face the darker side of the Internet. This title was even given to the name of my book in 2016 (Knibbs, 2016). The very fact that I used the term cybertrauma to denote the impact of online harm suggests that it's not all good. Many people regularly hear my keynotes and training about the dark side of people when it comes to the use of online spaces. Yet this technology is one of my most favourite things in my life.

DOI: 10.4324/9781032617251-8

POSITIVES ALL THE WAY!

Because technology has afforded us a way in which we can communicate with so many people, in so many ways, what this has allowed for is maintaining and making connections when normally we might not have the geographical, practical space, or time to do so. So many of my older clients will say in therapy that they wish they had spent more time with friends, which includes writing to them, calling them more, and visiting them (as many of them did not have this kind of technology with which to contact people). If we take the example of the year 2020 it is perhaps a grandiose statement to say that technology may well have prevented several, if not lots, of suicides related to loneliness, and that very technology might well have been our saving grace during lockdown.

I am aware this is not the case for everybody, especially those where social inclusion issues meant they did not have the technology or the skills with which to use that technology. Yet when I listen to the surrounding narrative about what happened with the COVID-19 virus, the very fact people used terms like zoom fatigue (Kuhn, 2022), say they are fed up with video meetings, and now appreciate the work life balance more than before lockdown, indicates that this technology was used to the point of that very fatigue.

It is suggested, although I cannot find any research to back up my claim here, that even homeless people were able to use technology during the time of lockdown (which is quite impressive and also suggests about the affordability of technology in today's world).

I give lectures around topics such as the disconnection of self in a world of technology connections, and for young people there is an evolving process of knowing that connection is always there, they don't even use the same terminology as the pre-internet 'boomer' crowd comparing on and offline settings. The space of connection is around them like a cloud and people are much more than imaginary figures in their heads. We are always reachable which can be soothing to know you are there for others or others are there for you (this might have its downsides too). I can see the positive to knowing the world is now borderless and within reach (metaphorically, metaphysically, and meta-cognitive(ly)). That feeling of waiting to know if someone of value has seen you and knows you're there has now become a reality that can lasts a lifetime. Moreover, if you want to hide from someone you can use the technology to 'bring up the shields!'.

COMMUNICATION

We are social creatures, surrounded by technology that allows for many more social interactions to take place (Turkle, 2015). The changing face of our social interactions now means that we can communicate in short texts emphasising feelings and intonation with little icons of faces things or grammatical images (Kaye, 2017). We can use a media format that allows us to see faces of the people we are conversing with and allows us to change those very faces with software additions such as filters and even the movement of our eyes toward the camera (invoking the feeling of being looked at) (https://www.nvidia.com/en-gb/geforce/news/jan-2023-nvidia-broadcast-update/).

Language

Language has allowed us the complexity of communication and nuance, and with each country or regions dialect providing us with a plethora of ways to describe the world we live in. Yet, language is now an evolving form of communication which can be (online) space specific (in-chat dialogue, gaming terms, for example) and even platform specific, for example the good old days of MSN nudges, once upon a time transitioned to Facebook and then removed. Institutions of varying forms (prison, the military, families for example) often have their own language and it would seem the online space is no different as a worldwide institution, which has allowed for our ability to understand where we are and what we're doing using such language. For example, 'meet you in the lobby' could signify that we are in a (real world) hotel and about to head somewhere else, but I suspect that most young people would know this means to be online in a specific game environment at an agreed time, with certain apps on and ready (e.g. Discord).

Cyber synapses

Our ability to connect with each other in these spaces allows for contact via cyber synapses in the same way that social connection occurs in a corporeal world (Knibbs, 2022a) when our energy is transmitted within and between (face to face interactions). We have adapted, albeit exceedingly quickly, to be mostly able to do this in the online world. What connection (in and through cyber space) provides for the inner psyche is, is a feeling of belonging, importance, and acknowledgement of our existence. A reply to a text, or post, message e-mail, or action within a gaming environment reinforces and maintains that acknowledgement and satiates our connection hunger. We have an always-on hive-mind, bringing emergent properties with the content transferred between the cyber synapses in the same way a brain evolves knowledge through energy and information flow (Knibbs, 2022a).

STROKE ECONOMIES ARE EASIER TO BALANCE

In transactional analysis the term stroke economy refers to the number of interactions that we require (per hour, per day, or over time), to meet connection and contact hunger (Berne, 1964). Strokes are the conditional and unconditional transactions that take place to meet those needs, and these can be positive or negative interactions. Online we can meet our quota *within minutes* if needs be. What the online space provides by the numbers of vast connections means that we can collect our strokes by the bucket full (quickly too).

This is quite a marvellous feat of ingenuity by creating spaces to connect. Knowing there is this number of connections available 24–7–365, it is no wonder that people want to spend their time in these online spaces finding a positive connection where that hunger can be satiated if it is missing 'out here' (Knibbs, 2022b).

Moreover, as technology becomes more immersive the way in which our brains decodes those interactions will become more like corporeal interactions. Whilst this has a scary element, this ability to feel within our own bodies that *we are with* the person we are talking to, who might be on the other side of the world for example, is only going to increase how that interaction feels on a visceral and psyche level.

SHYNESS, AUTISM AND SOCIALLY AWKWARD (PENGUINS)

A positive aspect about the ability to connect online is the example of a child (or adult) who might be shy, have a diagnosis of autism, struggle with social interactions, have verbal fluency difficulties, or perhaps a speech related issue such as a stutter is that there are so many ways to connect nowadays that these children, and adults, can now explore relational contact in a way that gives them agency, autonomy, and control over the situation (Shalkwyk et al., 2020). This is so different to the days gone by where children might have been pushed into a social group and told to get on with it. Knowing these children and adults can explore how to make and keep friends, without feeling like their nervous system is going to explode out of their body or crumple them to a heap of tears, is such a positive impact.

THE DEVELOPMENT OF A 'MWE'

Dan Siegel coined this term meaning when you have a me and a me and create an interpersonal connection then you create a 'Mwe' (Siegel, 2022). Cyberspace connections result in people being connected and young people and adults tell me that in the spaces where they go online, the communities they are part of often help them feel like they are with people who understand them, see them, and have the same interests etc. This can help them when they feel alone, in need of support, perhaps even reaching out to the therapist online who can help them feel they are seen by another person and in doing so feel part of a Mwe. Communities help us create a bigger Mwe, and taking what Jamie Wheal (2021) talks about as Communitas we can create the church and state of the future. I am sure that during lockdown many of these spaces existed, and still do today.

Loneliness is suggested to be one of the biggest killers of human beings (Heinrich & Gullone, 2006) more than health conditions related to smoking, cardiovascular issues, etc., and so having spaces where social connections can take place such as social media or gaming has the potential to reduce these mortality figures. As we move into the future and this technology becomes more integrated and more like the corporeal interactions that we have I suspect that people will find more connections that can help reduce loneliness.

MOTABILITY, DISABILITY, AND REMOTE AREAS

This connection to others can also be a positive for people who are limited physically to a location such as a house, perhaps because they have a disability, or motability issue, or perhaps live in a remote area where physical contact with other human beings is limited. This technology affords connections via borderless spaces in the online world outside of immediate family, occupational therapists, or medical staff visiting for example. This can also be useful for people who want to engage in a therapeutic process and may be limited or prevented by the anxiety of leaving the house. A well-trained online therapist can provide a much-needed mental health respite space (Anthon & Nagel, 2010).

BELONGINGNESS

When it comes to connections in an online community such as gaming this can and does enhance a feeling of belonging and like-mindedness with others who may share our passions and likes (Allen,

2021). This often cements one of the most important internal processes that we have as social creatures. Moreover, this can provide a space that is fun, engaging, and gives us a reason to want to be with others. When taking part in gaming environments we can see that cohesion, reciprocity, turn taking, skill building, cooperation, and mastery can all be enhanced and supported by others, and in doing so can be facilitated by humour, gentle teasing, and team building. Group connection is as important as a one-to-one interaction as human beings operate in both small and large group dynamics, and most gaming environments allow the person to control what level of group number they encounter. Establishing friend groups is an imperative part of development of the human being and gaming environments most certainly provide much of this (Bean, 2018).

SCAFFOLDING, COORDINATION, AND OTHER SKILLS

Gaming not only provides a community space but one in which a person can begin to develop skills beyond their comfort range, sometimes scaffolded by others helping. These skills will include thinking, planning, reasoning, fine motor movements (if they use a controller or keyboard and mouse), and much larger movements such as coordination, for example when using the Wii, Kinect, and virtual reality, which can be helpful with physical difficulty movements. For example, many of the children I work with have coordination issues such as dyspraxia and being able to game, using many varieties of platforms or environments, enables what we call bilateral communication, which can help with nervous system regulation, balance, and of course an improvement in coordination (sometimes).

EMOTIONAL REGULATION

Gaming can help with (even though it doesn't seem so sometimes), emotional regulation, distress tolerance, frustration, and a tenacity for giving it another go which is referred to in literature as having grit and determination (Bean, 2018; Duckworth, 2017). Gaming also seems (without robust research to back this up) to provide a faster attentional and cognitive processing of energy and information being interacted with compared to a conversation with another person face to face. When you look at the speed of choices being made in a fast-paced game, with 120 bits of information or more on a number of screens at any one time it is outstanding how this can all be processed, especially by children who seem to do this much faster than adults (and most certainly me). This speed of processing is remarkable to witness, and I wonder if the capabilities and evolution of our cognition systems is improving. Perhaps this is why the world is boring to a brain that can move so fast, and this may be one of the reasons why attentional focus seems to be attributed to a mental health disorder that is on the rise? A side question here: I wonder how many people read through this book in one go to get it finished quickly, or listened to it sped up on an audio version?

EDUCATION: THE RISE OF COOKING?

A very quick little tangent here is to talk about the educational purposes of gaming. Whilst I could sit and talk about many of the games that children play that can help them learn about facts and figures, history, science, and more I thought I would give a quick reflection on a game that a client of mine several years ago used to play on their tablet. It encouraged a passion for cooking and baking and resulted in the child developing language and common knowledge and skills around baking, and as a result one of the joyful tasks we enjoyed together in the therapy office was decorating the cakes that my client had baked. At the age of eight or nine years of age they went on to win a baking award, beating adults in the same class! They were incredibly proud, and these have been some of the best buns I've decorated (okay… eaten). Especially given they were created by a young child using technology to facilitate an interest and hobby, and I hope to see them on Bake Off or an equivalent show in the years to come, this was their dream.

I've watched many streamers also playing games that involve cooking, serving up plates of food, working alongside the chef, cleaning up and running a business, which can't be a bad side effect to playing a game if it helps establish the understanding of running a business. Games by proxy provide a learning environment. If you want to understand the kinds of games that you can play as a family or with your child, then head over to www.taminggaming.com. It is the largest database of games to date for families and read *A Parent's Guide to Video Games* (Kowert, 2016).

GAMING AND THE FLOW STATE

Often when we hear about the flow state it is often a very brief description in a book about the skills-challenge sweet spot (or channel as it's often called). It is a state of consciousness and is an extremely large topic outside of gaming and this book, so I intend to keep this simple here for the word count, but suggest that you can read more on Csikszentmihalyi (1992/2002) in his books and through organisations that teach about this topic such as the ones that have helped me, The Flow Genome Project (https://www.flowgenomeproject.com/), and the Flow Research Collective (https://www.flowresearchcollective.com/). The flow state also has a large body of evidence behind it in terms of neurobiology and psychology and why we are drawn to engage in processes that can help us connect to our best selves. What gaming provides when it comes to flow is a state that is referred to as selflessness, timelessness, effortlessness, and having a richness to it. Immersed in a task that is challenging, and often playful, and removes that nagging inner voice is said to be an autotelic process, meaning we want to do it again and again. This is where a person is said to be in a state of temporal hypo frontality (timeless and lacking a sense of me), which means that we are within and on task in a state of attention like no other. It is said the flow state produces a cocktail of six neurotransmitters all at once, which by design creates a feeling within us of wanting to re-enter this state for no other reason than how it feels (https://www.flowresearchcollective.com/). Children are often in this state in the here and now, but certainly it feels like they reach this state faster than adults when gaming. And in my line of work in trauma, flow is the antithesis of this distressing state. The nervous system is blissful in flow and as an 'antidote' to trauma this is one of the reasons (child) therapists play and use play therapy for trauma (Goodyear-Brown, 2019). I have found computer games as well as physical corporeal games to be as useful in the healing of trauma, so I am very much in their favour professionally.

SINGULAR OR GROUP FLOW

This is us at our best, being our best, and feeling our best in a controllable environment. This drive often underpins people who are high state seeking, often called adrenaline seekers, in high-risk maximum-reward hobbies like extreme sports. Gaming provides many of the facets required for flow and in doing so the desire to return to the game is both facilitated by cognitive aspects of wanting to achieve mastery and skill such as completion of levels perhaps, or a puzzle within the game. When looking at group flow (Kotler & Wheal, 2018) this can easily be seen in the way that online gaming platforms connect several people in one space, where communication during the game produces flow and communication in this state and can become almost telekinetic. A shared experience and understanding with a well-defined goal and outcome – specific, clear, and smart – can easily produce what are called the flow triggers for such a group experience.

FOUR PERCENT: HOW THE GAMING INDUSTRY PROVIDES THIS FOR EACH PERSON

When a person plays a game, the challenge and the skills required for that challenge meet the requirements for the flow when these are slightly above a person's skill level and competency. Rising to the challenge for flow requires it is slightly beyond boredom and less than anxiety inducing, the skills required are just beyond what is required, and both factors sit at approximately 4% above what is, let's call it 'everyday normal' (whatever that means) (Kotler, 2021). I find flow ebbs or increases depending on the task required and what mood I'm in which impedes or pushes the struggle aspect of the flow cycle. They provide sufficient challenge that a person wants to engage in the task, it's neither too complicated nor mundane. Gaming companies have created many differing types of games to meet these differing skills of people who play, and this is why understanding *what* a game is, what *type* of game, the *modus operandi for playing*, and the *skills required* for the challenges within can help us understand why they are important for a person. And if it is true that all humans seek the flow state wherever possible, then the world of gaming is providing a much-needed state of consciousness, and respite from everyday toils and stresses and supports creativity. If we think about the children who play these games and their ability to increase their skills and complexity in differing challenges, then imagine how their thinking can be supported in a positive direction rather than seeing it as a detrimental impact or 'making children dumber', which is the common narrative. The flow state often enables expertise in a short time.

GAMIFICATION AND HELPING PEOPLE IN EDUCATION, EMPLOYMENT, AND MENTAL HEALTH

Using principles of play, gaming, sports, and competition has produced a term and action called gamification. It is often used in settings where encouragement to engage in an activity is required. This might be for example in schools where points are handed out for the best drawing, group project, or sports day league tables, or in work settings where KPI results are paid a bonus, and in therapeutic settings where a person might take on a 'crusade' to conquer an internalised parent. The gamification applies to the domains of cognition, emotion, social, relational, and psychological aspects. It is utilised in this way because gaming, flow are a harmonious pair that enable *play and learning* to take place. This taps into one's desire to *do better* or *be better* and it might be said to *get better*. We all do this and a game I suspect you have gamified is 'Beat the GPS ETA'. Yep, me too (legally of course).

REAL WORLD GAMING: SUPERBETTER AND SUPER, BETTER!

One of my favourite recommendations for clients is the process that a psychologist called Jane McGonigal (2015) created. A game called Superbetter with these gamification characteristics as a way for people to improve their mental health and move forward out of issues like depression or anxiety. She uses the exact same criteria and processes of gaming and bringing that into the corporeal world to enable people to play their own version of a game. Many parents engage in this, for example think about the 'ready steady go' phrase used in racing your child to clean up their toys, and or how parents can create playful games so that the toy box is tidied up. Gaming which includes gamification of real-world events produces a shared understanding and playful connection that allows a regulatory-relational process to take place. In the example above a child can feel seen and important which will also produce the same chemicals of bonding and attachment that are present in the flow state. This is one of the reasons why young children use the phrase 'again again!'.

GAMING, JOY, AND MEANINGFULNESS

Gaming can produce joyful feelings (and yes those frustrating ones too), but ask a person if they want to stop a frustrating game and they often say no I am (actually) having fun. What we certainly know within the spaces of mental health diagnoses is that joy can often be in deficit much of the time, for example with a person who suffers with depression. In my therapy clinic, on my TikTok posts, and in communities online people suffering with mental health disorders often reflect that gaming is a lifeline, escape from their issue, or provides them with some purpose. When we look to the rates of suicide behaviour often people will reflect on a lack of meaningfulness and purpose in life.

I have found (anecdotally) with many clients, over many years that gaming has helped with medical issues, life limiting illnesses, life threatening illnesses such as cancer, mental health issues such as depression, and has provided a much-needed space where my clients have stated it is the only thing that kept them going.

GAMERS BEAT CANCER: THE GIFT OF GAMING[2]

In 2023 Steven Bracewell, founder of GBC died from this disease, and I wanted to honour what he envisioned and why. At the outset of GBC, he wanted people with cancer to be supported using gaming in the same way he and other members of GBC had found solace, peace, and connection in their time in palliative spaces.

At the outset of GBC, Steven, his wife Debbie, Ben Nicholls and I, set out to have conversations with people in healthcare and beyond about how we could support cancer patients and their families. Steven wanted to create communities and provide the *gift of gaming* to people in these spaces. I wanted to interview him for a book to explore this in depth, but sadly 2023 was not a great time for his diagnosis with his battle of 'the biggest boss' as we jokingly called it; sadly it was not to be and so I must rely on the conversations and recording we did. The charity (as it now is), is very successful at providing people with gaming equipment to support them through the most traumatic or difficult times of their lives and it still needs to grow (sorry Debs for the admin that will follow!). In short people with a diagnosis, receiving chemo, or relatives can apply for consoles and adaptations for equipment if treatment has changed their bodily functions. Waiting and time in hospitals or hospices are long and arduous. If this helps one person manage their time and provides a space to be positive about their treatment, then Steve achieved what he set out to. Debbie, Andy Berry, and Dave Wright are currently meeting the needs of the GOG community so please either donate money to buy stuff, tell people about them, give them your old consoles for distribution to the GOG and support the work they do. There is still more to do under Steve's legacy.

People in distress and through GBC have told me they relied on gaming as much as they did oxygen in the air. When a person tells you that gaming is so important in this way it really shows how important this space really is. I'm not sure we would ever talk about medication in the punitive way that we do about gaming. Gaming can be that good for the soul and for a person and it provided Steve with a gaming community and people and that included social media groups too. This is the link to what that GBC did in lockdown with Steve in hospital (the fundraising videos are 18+) and you can find them on the internet too on social media no less (https://gamers-beatcancer.co.uk/).

NOTES

1 https://www.youtube.com/watch?v=u6woaSJTMFU.
2 https://gamersbeatcancer.co.uk/.

8

HOW CAN TECHNOLOGY IMPROVE MENTAL HEALTH?

EXPLANATIONS FIRST

How can we use technology to help us not use technology? Is this a contradiction, catch 22, or is this a double-edged sword of being in the environment that is creating the issue? Am I suggesting the equivalent of sending an alcoholic into a bar or nightclub? What you will gain from this chapter is how to set your device, computer, or environment for intentional use of technology. Not everyone has the cash flow to have specific devices for specific functions and all apps on one device is the digital distraction we can often fall foul of. So how can we 'use' tech positively?

We are aiming to do the opposite of what you might call excessive screen time, addiction, too much gaming, doom scrolling, or FOMO. We want to engage with our technology intentionally and when we have the capacity to do so mentally, or time wise.

In Chapter 5 (on helping yourself), I discussed writing down your behaviours (these were the noticing exercises). The reason for this is that when we engage our motor movement system, that is using our hand to write, we are more engaged in the *task at hand* (I've got to stop using these puns) (Planton et al., 2013). What I could have asked you to do, and did not, was suggested that you used an app to be able to track the behaviours, feelings, or thoughts. Why?

DOI: 10.4324/9781032617251-9

Because you might have been doing that task when a quick thought about 'I'll just check Instagram, emails or WhatsApp' pops into your head, because the same device to do these things is in your hand. It's a subtle, curated association of needs and feelings in your subconscious when 'it' is in your hand.

WHAT DO WE *WANT* TO DO?

We're going to use some positive apps and ways of understanding ourselves that can counteract those nudges, pings, and algorithms that suggest to us that this is what we really really really want, Zig A Zig… arghh!!

MIND-FULL-NESS, NOT MIND-LESS-NESS

Often in therapeutic settings people are introduced to disciplines and paradigms of mindfulness (Hanh, 2008), also known as being present, in the here and now. And I'm sure if you ask any mindfulness teacher on the planet, they will tell you that this is a particularly difficult space-time continuum to inhabit for more than a few minutes at a time before you time travel with thoughts or distractions. So, let's address what this means. Often, we are so caught up with our own internal time travel, remembering things that have happened, things that we did or didn't do, people we spoke to, places we've been etc., that we are caught up in the past. Conversely, we can be projecting, considering what's going to happen, what might happen, and all the things we have the potential and possibility for, in the future.

In mindfulness the approach is to be in the present and when you are in this space you are neither here nor there, in the past or the future. This is one of the ways we can hugely support our mental health because our problems lie in the past and in the future, and few in the here and now (Williams & Penman, 2011). If we are noticing something in the here and now it's more than likely it's associated with something in the past propelling a response. But noticing and not reacting, ah that is exactly where the language of 'zen' comes in.

I'm going to invite you to engage with mindfulness, the discipline to give you more skills in the domain of responses and reactions and choice. These are the foundation of awareness and action and being in control of that action. If more people did this proactively, deliberately, and with full intention, the spaces online and in people's nervous systems would provide us all with a less reactive and polarised planet. Compassion and empathy would be a driving force of good for us and others.

It sounds easy, on paper. But online?

The tech companies want us to be anything other than mindful, otherwise the *spells* won't work.

Some of the following suggestions may not be for you. They may feel excessively uncomfortable, bring up feelings of distress or anxiousness and as a trauma therapist it is my clinical duty of care to inform you that mediation, breathwork, closing your eyes, and journaling may need the assistance of a well trained professional to support you. I am aware there are protocols, advice, and content online from 'Bro science' as well as actual research studies telling you to do these things, but…

This is your choice and knowledge of your own body-rules here, not my suggestions. You know you better than I do, and it would be irresponsible to tell you to do things where I do not have your history to hand to make informed decisions for you. This happens way too often online, with qualified PhDs, GPs and MDs doing this to an audience they cannot see or know. Clout hunting over ethics? I see the longer-term damage it can cause.

Everything in this chapter is an invitation not an instruction.

Primum Non Nocere: First do no harm.[1]

TikTok advice I am not.

DEMYSTIFYING THE MAGIC

I would like to invite you to purposefully think about using an app that can help you develop the skill to be in the present moment, more often, and with awareness. There are many on the market and I have no affiliation with any of them, however one of the largest apps, used by many people and one I recommend wholeheartedly is the app called 'waking up' by Sam Harris and others (https://www.wakingup.com/). You can use this link https://www.wakingup.com/cath for a free month trial and find out if you like it. On this app there are numerous timed, silent, and narrated meditations and plenty of theory from which to learn about this discipline. As I was writing this, I noticed that the word meditation might have jarred with some readers. This is not the same as mindfulness, but a type of exercise within the discipline, even though you are mindful in the mediation (Goleman & Davidson, 2018). If that makes sense? It often conjures up an image of a yogi, sitting on a cushion singing ohm, and if you wish to do this, that's also a form of mindful mediation so go for it, if that's your thing.

SCIENCE OF MINDFULNESS

What neuroscience tells us (remembering what I've said about research and what we do know and what we can know), is pretty much mind-full-ness, it is often what's really happening in our heads almost continuously. We tend to spend our time thinking, planning, worrying, remembering, and each interaction on social media or gaming can spark a wave of thoughts and associations to the memories we hold in our heads. We disconnect from our bodies and being present, and spend that time interacting with the media we are looking at, whatever we have in our heads (or not), for what can seem like hours. This is one of the reasons why we get 'caught up' in the scrolling because we are mind-less of our mind-full, and lacking in the mind-here-and-now-ness. Being able to avoid these traps requires us to become skilled *at noticing* and this is why the exercises are in the book, and in mindful mediation practices. They are called practices because they require continuous practice.

PRACTICE APPS AND TECH SPACES

Eyes closed

You might want to use a different app such as headspace (https://www.headspace.com/), insight timer (https://insighttimer.com/en-gb), and another lovely one is syntropy (https://www.syntropystates.com/). When I make recommendations for any app or platform within my practice, I check on the United Kingdom that it passes under the Orcha (https://orchahealth.com/) set of standards for data protection privacy and appropriateness for people that I work with. Here I am suggesting apps that are not directly prescribed by NHS clinicians and you might want to spend some time looking for an app that might work for you (notice how long this takes you too). You can even find videos that help you on YouTube. Perhaps you might want to create your own list of apps and videos or audios that work for you in helping you become present, aware, able to notice, and non-judgmental.

Eyes open

Moreover, in the world of virtual reality there are some apps that have been developed to enable you to explore mindfulness, meditation, and awareness practises. For example, Spirit VR (https://www.scenegraphstudios.com/portfolio/spiritvr-journey-vr-mental-wellbeing/) (developed by a company I work with) is a simple breath awareness, body scan, and mindfulness meditation app which is immersive and is very much a different experience, compared to listening to a narrated version that you complete by yourself in the corporeal world.

Other apps that exist in the VR/XR environment are ones such as Tripp (https://www.tripp.com/), Liminal (https://liminalvr.com/), Flow VR (sitting at the side of an Icelandic Mountain or lake) (https://www.flow.is/)[s], and others which also introduce something called biofeedback such as Deep VR (https://www.exploredeep.com/). As I write this paragraph, I am aware of more being developed and can certainly say from my own practise that using these immersive meditation apps have a different qualia to them. Trying to describe that qualitatively here for someone who has never tried VR would be like trying to describe a food you've never tasted. *An attempt to do this*: imagine that you are sitting in space with the most miraculous colours and scenery in a 360 degree area, that you can interact with, with your controllers (or hands), and audio music and voices that are timed with the images and colours.

THE ORIGINAL GANGSTER (OG) MEDITATOR

That might give you a hint as to what exists in the space of new and developing technology. However, I'm sure the long-standing meditator would (possibly) say all that distraction takes away from the mindfulness aspect of meditation and so it is not entirely how these practises were developed originally. But we don't live in 'original times'. We now have exciting interactive media developments that can enable people who find mediation and mindfulness practices difficult, a way to engage with the practice. This is a way, not *the only* way, to engage with the practice. Horses for courses as the saying goes. Find what works for you.

Breathwork: it isn't all Wim, or Grof

Breath work has gained quite the following in the online spaces, thanks to celebs like Wim Hof (https://www.wimhofmethod.com/), TV shows, podcasts, and insta gurus (often in cold plunge 'groups'). This intervention, for me, requires a deep understanding of the impact of each type of practise, and how it affects the body and nervous system before I use this with a client (it has taken me years to learn this stuff). I wish more people did this before asking other people (clients, customers, or patients) to engage in breath work because it's trendy and they saw Wim Hof online. It can retraumatise a person's nervous system, and so my caveat here is: this may be another exercise that is not for you; your choice and knowledge of your own body rules here not my suggestions.

Again, there are many apps that can help with breath work, my favourite is one called Othership (https://othership.com/) (I can send you a free month to try if you email me). Many of the exercises on this app are high intensity versions in comparison to many of the Heart Rate Variability services I use in therapy and trauma work. Breathing has the potential to impact your nervous system more quickly than any other intervention. This is why people will often ask you to 'breathe calmly' when in distress, why birthing protocols involve specific forms of breathing, and special forces use this for changing their state rapidly (and people who want to get high on their own supply). But it's also the intervention that can provoke anxiety, dissociation, and feelings of panic in some people. This is a cautionary tale of using a process that you might not like but one in which mastery is achievable. Coherent breathing is said to centre your body through the three centres of brain, heart, and gut (https://www.heartmath.com/).

Breath of life: skills, mastery, and broad application

This for me forms a part of mindfulness meditation and this can be an addition to mindfulness or a separate process within itself. You might be thinking how or why is breathwork included in this chapter, and the simplest explanation is that it exists as a process that helps you become aware of your body in the here and now, can elevate your state of consciousness, provide a trigger for flow, and most importantly is a self-regulatory exercise. I wonder how much notice you paid to your breath when reading these paragraphs? We often don't pay attention to our breath, and we want to be able to manage ourselves *before the technology does this for us* so to speak. The technology apps and the exercises here can help us centre and be present, before we use our devices, games, and social media. And it can help way beyond the tech too.

Emotional tracking

The positive steps we can take above and beyond mindfulness and breathing are (using apps or platforms that can help us) tracking our emotional ups and downs during the day, and how you might rate these emotions, what we call valence. This can help you notice how these interact with and after your online or gaming activities. For example, you can access apps that can help you track how you are feeling, often called mood trackers, and help you develop your emotional quotient lexicon, that is, your language skills about your emotions to help you identify what it is you're feeling and name it (Goleman, 1995). We call this emotional intelligence, and it relates to discrete emotion theories (Eckman, 2004). A surprising fact for many of my clients is there are approximately 300 known and distinct emotions (Barrett et al., 2016). They have some basic characteristics such as active versus passive and pleasurableness (or not) and the leading voice in research about emotions and their impact on the body (budget) is Lisa Feldman Barrett (2018).

Why is it important to track emotions? In short this helps us see what impact things in our lives have upon us. You may notice that you track a feeling of sadness before or after using your device every Sunday evening. This sadness could be due to the knowledge that you are due back at work tomorrow, and when you compare this to your screentime numbers, you may start to notice that sadness equals more time online on Sunday evenings, or more time online equals sadness on a Sunday. You may notice particular apps have an impact on particular emotions. For example, using facetime with friends seems to 'boost your mood' and spending time on TikTok has it crashing down the longer you spend on it. As I said in earlier chapters, we can see the links between emotions such as loneliness and time online, or our needs and emotions driving that time online. Emotions may be easier for you to track. Information is power with which to change your habits!

JOURNALING: MORNING, NOON, OR NIGHT

There are apps that can help you engage in a process called journaling, which is also suggested to be a positive benefit exercise for that noticing and awareness (Ullrich & Lutgendorf, 2002). Perhaps you would like to write down about your use of games or social media and how you feel about them in a journal. Many of these exist in app format and most phones have a notes app too that you could use. My question here would be whether typing out your feelings (or writing out) is something you could fit into your day and at what time? Not every intervention is suitable for every person, and one element of awareness ever present in my mind is: not all of us live in safe spaces. By that I mean children who use journals often hide them from prying eyes of parents or siblings. As adults we are no different really, wanting to keep our thoughts private. There may be some readers who are in relationships that may not allow for this kind of privacy, and perhaps writing down one's thoughts can feel extremely exposing or can be used by others to hurt and ridicule us. We may want to password protect our journal systems, which often you cannot do with pen and paper.

What we notice when journaling: our patterns. Those patterns can be illuminating about something that might be repetitive in our life or interrupting us or preventing us from living the life that we want. Although awareness of this patterning is often not enough in itself to make those changes it can help us see what we do, how and when. The discovery from herein is the why.

GESTALT AND THE FINISHING OF TASKS

As you're reading through these positive interventions, apps, processes, and exercises you might be noticing that they utilise the same mechanisms that we use in those spaces of social media and gaming. For many of us, conscious and purposeful use of a tool is empowering, whereas finding ourselves scrolling on an app for much longer than we intended can feel less than empowering, and often leaves us feeling frustrated, distressed, or annoyed that we've spent that time looking at stuff that really isn't that important. For those who game longer than they initially intended they may not have been aware, or totally aware in many cases, of the need to complete a task in the game and get to the next save point or complete the match for example.

This need to complete a task, a gestalt (Mann,2020) is a drive that 'most folk have'. This desire to finish a process, a book, a film, that Netflix box set, that level, that game, that puzzle, and so on can feel almost compulsive. Now when you see, usually in mainstream media articles or blogs, podcasts or YouTube videos, the discussions around Attention Deficit Hyperactivity Disorder (ADHD) (Koutsoklenis & Honkasilta, 2023) and the *not finishing of tasks* you might be thinking here that the gestalt only applies to non-ADHD persons. This is not true, and we need much more research into this diagnosis and time spent online, gaming, or with tasks etc. as it seems that the hyperfocus of attentional type diagnosis has a number of these folk finishing a game way before those without the diagnosis; i.e. there are several gamers who play new games at Christmas solidly within three days to complete the campaign or story. This strikes me as counter intuitive to the diagnosis as according to the manuals these symptoms are present in every domain (apart from gaming?).

Being aware of our own need to complete a task can give us some insight into why we might for example be scrolling for much longer than we intended, a little like the itch that doesn't leave after being scratched. Many young people I speak to have an awareness of this feeling when they are online, social media, gaming but often lack the knowledge about what to do with this feeling or behaviour and so find themselves at the mercy of the big tech behavioural economic bear trap. Perhaps you're reading this, and you know the feeling I'm talking about. This 'leaving something unfinished' can feel uncomfortable and is a technique I learned when writing books. It is the hook that reels me back in, to complete a sentence paragraph or page of writing. That unfinished feeling 'bugs me' and that's the intention of leaving a sentence half.

SO HOW CAN YOU USE TECHNOLOGY TO BEAT THE BEAR TRAP?

Only open the apps when you are intentional about their use. Be disciplined.

Or...

Use tech to beat tech. One device for all occasions or use programmes to intercept your habits.

It is completely optional for you to use these software interventions as many companies are trying to help us all beat the bear trap. There are courses dedicated to avoiding digital distractions if you want to achieve optimal performance whilst using the devices in which you could be distracted in, from, or with.

Discipline seems to be something that's associated with weight training, running, or working hard if you listen to any podcasts or people online (Clear, 2018). And I know we live in a world of quick fixes, rather then tapping into our own willpower and so this section has a list of companies and software to help you hack that willpower and distraction. What these companies cannot do, and why I have written this book in this way, is to help you understand your needs and wants and why you use tech like you do.

For that there is no quick fix and perhaps reading Allan De Botton's (2023) book is a good start for giving you some tips on the inner child work that you may need to do. I can help you with that outside of the book contents, so do check my website (for workshop dates and availability) if that's an option you wish to take up (www.childrenandtech.co.uk).

QUICK HACK HITS: BUILD NEW HABITS!

Read or listen to some of the books such as *A Distracted Mind* (Gazzelay & Rosen, 2016), *Atomic Habits* (Clear, 2018), *Hooked* (Eyal, 2014), *Indestractible* (Eyal, 2020), *Mindset Changing* (Dweck, 2017), *Unsubscribe* (Glei, 2016), *Digital Minimalism* (Newport, 2019) (and others by Cal Newport), *The Craving Mind* (Brewer, 2018), and anything with 'dopamine' or 'digital' and 'detox' in the title. Those last two are said with a weary bow of my head, because they might just work and so are listed. I don't agree with all of the books here, but this is not about me, it's about what works for you.

You could watch lectures listed below, and no I do not agree with all of them either, or everything said in them, but they may be exactly what you need to hear, and it is a much more time savvy decision to watch these than read a long book for some people. Watch out that you don't consume more than you intend to as they are YouTube links and remember, it's easy to watch the next video, and the next etc!

WEB BLOCKERS, TIME LIMITATIONS, AND MORE

There are some great pieces of software that exist in the world of beating the bear trap and helping you become more focused when using your tech. Some help with email filtering and you can ask your email client to do this for you, or you can buy others such as unroll me (https://unroll.me/) (not available in the EU) or inbox when ready. If you want to limit your time and access to websites when you're working you can use newsfeed eradicator (https://chromewebstore.google.com/detail/newsfeed-eradicator-20/clfonknljamomadgkcciofnhfegjinhd), self-control (https://selfcontrolapp.com/), or parental control software. If you want to limit time on apps you can also use parental control software for yourself or your child, and other apps that might be called productivity and focusing types, such as digital wellbeing (by Google), screentime (by Apple), Rescue time (https://www.rescuetime.com/), Forest (https://www.forestapp.cc/) (I love the gamification in this one and the idea of growing trees, pity it's not real ones), freedom (https://freedom.to/), and flipd (https://www.flipdapp.co/). I am sure there are others, but this list is the one I hand to my clients.

(Quick tip: If you want to aid yourself here, using some of the guidelines you'll find online move your apps on a smartphone to separate pages or screens, with games and social media furthest from the home screen. In VR and Console apps I'm afraid you will need to find your own way to replicate this idea because I don't know what system you are using and could be here all day trying to describe how to do this/that on Xbox, Occulus or PlayStation consoles. On PC install software that can limit times you can access certain apps or websites and create folders with apps in for one purpose and one file folder for mindful videos, audio tracks or apps.)

Or you could, if you have the money and desire to do this, buy a phone or device for specific purposes. For example, a kindle for reading, a smartphone for social media, a laptop for writing, and a computer for working from home and meetings. I know this may seem indulgent, but this follows the principle of one environment to work in, one to play in, and one to get some admin completed, in a similar way to 'going to the office, the gym, the garden and the beach'. Each one has a purpose and keeping the purpose in that environment alone is good for productivity. However, I know many people have TVs with video on demand services on as well as the cable channels, and it's this TV that hosts the console games when turned on. And we know how much TV has ruined the evenings of many people around the world, by giving us a space to flop on the sofa and binge on rubbish, especially in holiday seasons!

Whatever you choose to do, or use, is up to you. Technology can help us interfere with the tech companies plans and give us back some of our time. Maybe you are happy knowing your why from the previous chapters and don't feel the need to use technology, apps, or software and want to engage in learning how to be present and notice your internal landscape and weather pattern to beat the bear trap. Technology can help in positive ways as I described above and all the educational or joyful content we consume online is one of the reasons we use it as much as we do.

Noting the positives may help you see it's not all wasted time online, much to the current narrative of its negative media, over there… (wanting you to consume their content; talk about hypocritical). Joy and learning are such an important part of our development and emotional wellbeing. Keeping negative emotions and behaviours at bay, permanently, is impossible, so learn to be compassionate with yourself. And wouldn't you know there's an app for that too! And books, online courses, and lectures as well, just saying.

YOUTUBE LECTURES

Tame your distracted mind (https://www.youtube.com/watch?v=vNEoMXQloN8).

A powerful antidote to distraction (https://www.youtube.com/watch?v=GfXWAggwC-E).

Quit social media (https://www.youtube.com/watch?v=3E7hkPZ-HTk).

How social media ruins your life (https://www.youtube.com/watch?v=kc_Jq42Og7Q).

Why video games are so hard to put down (https://www.youtube.com/watch?v=T8tq0xiOwKI).

NOTE

1 http://classics.mit.edu/Hippocrates/epidemics.1.i.html.

SUGGESTIONS FOR FURTHER READING

Atrill-Smith, A., Fullwood, C., Keep, M., & Kuss, D. (2019). *The Oxford handbook of cyberpsychology*. Oxford University Press.

Ball, M. (2022). *The metaverse and how it will revolutionise everything*. Liveright Publishing Corporation.

boyd, d. (2014). *It's complicated: The social lives of networked teens*. Yale.

Culata, R. (2021). *Digital for good. Raising kids to thrive in an online world*. Harvard Business Review Press.

Duffy, J. (2019). *Parenting the new teen in the age of anxiety. A complete guide to your child's stressed, depress, expanded amazing adolescence*. Mango Publishing.

Etchells, P. (2024). *Unlocked: The real science of screentime and how to spend it better*. Piatkus.

Hanson, R. (2018). *Resilient. Find your inner strength*. Rider.

Hare, S. (2022). *Technology is not neutral. A short guide to technology ethics*. London Publishing Partnership.

Kardefelt-Winther, D., Rees G., & Livingstone, S. (2020). Contextualising the link between adolescents use of digital technology and their mental health: a multi country study of time spent online and life satisfaction. *Journal of Child Psychology and Psychiatry*, 61(8), 875–889.

Kelly, Y., Zilanawala, A., Booker, C., & Sacker, A. (2018). Social media use and adolescent mental health: findings from the UK Millennium Cohort Study. *EClinicalMedicine*, 6, 59–68.

Khasawneh, A., Madathil, C., Dixon E., Wisneiwski P., Zinzow H., & Roth R. (2020). Examining the self harm and suicide contagion effects of the blue whale challenge on YouTube and twitter: qualitative study. *JMIR Mental Health*, 7(6).

Lanier, J. (2018). *Ten arguments for deleting your social media accounts right now*. Bodley Head.

Martínez, V., Jiménez-Molina, Á., & Gerber, M. (2023). Social contagion, violence, and suicide among adolescents. *Current Opinion in Psychiatry*, 36(3), 237–242.

Memon, A., Sharma, S., Mohite, S., & Jain S. (2018). The role of online social networking on deliberate self harm and suicidality in adolescents. A systemized review of literature. *Indian Journal of Psychiatry*, 60(4), 384–392.

Merzencich, M. (2013). *Soft-wired. How the new science of brain plasticity can change your life*. Parnassus Publishing.

Orben, A., Dienlin, T., & Przybylski, A. (2019). Social media's enduring effect on adolescent life satisfaction. *Proceedings of the National Academy of Sciences of the United States of America*, 116, 10226–10228.

Rossi, G., & DeSilva, R. (2020), Social media applications a potential avenue for broadcasting suicide attempts and self injurious behaviour. *Cureus*, 12(10), 10759.

Sadagheyani, H., & Tatari, F. (2020). Investigating the role of social media on mental health. *Mental Health and Social Inclusion*, 25(1), 41–51.

Scott, D., Valley, B., & Simecka, B. (2017). Mental health concerns in the digital age. *International Journal of Mental Health and Addiction*, 15, 604–613.

Schønning, V., Hjetland, G., Aarø, L., & Skogen, J. (2020). Social media use and mental health and well-being among adolescents – a scoping review. *Frontiers in Psychology*, 11.

Stavrova, O., Denissen, J., & Denissen, J. (2020). Does using social media jeopardize well-being? The importance of separating within- from between-person effects. *Social Psychological and Personality Science*, 12, 964–973.

Turkle, S. (2016) *Reclaiming conversation: The power of talk in a digital age*. Penguin.

Turkle, S. (2017) *Alone together: Why we expect more from technology and less from each other*. Basic Books.

Valkenburg, P., Meier, A., & Beyens, I. (2021). Social media use and its impact on adolescent mental health: An umbrella review of the evidence. *Current Opinion in Psychology*, 44, 58–68.

Young, L., Kolubinski, D., & Frings, D. (2020). Attachment style moderates the relationship between social media use and user mental health and well-being. *Heliyon*, 6.

REFERENCES

INTRODUCTION

Knibbs, C. (2020). Compassion in cyberspace. In Irfan, Coles M. (ed.) *Education for survival. The pedagogy of compassion*. UCL Books.

Knibbs, C. (2021). Online harm, online living and the impact for children and young people. A conversation with Lisa Cherry. In Cherry, L. *Conversations that make a difference for children and young people*. Routledge.

Knibbs, C. (2022). *Bodies, brains and technology – The real social dilemma*. TEDx Doncaster. https://www.youtube.com/watch?v=lRX_DWo3KPs.

Knibbs, C. (2023). Ethics and cyberethics. In Knibbs, C. & Hibberd, G. (eds) *A practitioners guide to cybersecurity and data protection*. Routledge and MHVR International Coalition.

CHAPTER 1

Ace, Dick, P. (1962). *The man in the high castle*. Putnam.

Benson, R., Mcternan, N., Ryan, F., & Arensman, E. (2021). Suicide clustering and contagion. The Role of the media. *Suicidolgi* NR, 2.

Etchells, P. (2024). *Unlocked: The real science of screentime and how to spend it better*. Piatkus.

Gibson, W. (1984). *Neuromancer*. Gollancz.

Hare, S. (2022). *Technology is not neutral: A short guide to technology ethics*. London Publishing Partnership.

Heidegger, M. (1977). *The question concerning technology and other essays* (trans. W. Lovitt). Harper & Row. (Original works published 1952, 1954, 1962).

Huxley, A. (1932/1994). *Brave new world* . Vintage.

Knibbs, C. (2022). *Children, technology and healthy development*. Routledge.

Knibbs, C. (2023a). *Children and sexual based online harms*. Routledge.

Knibbs C. (2023b). *Cybertrauma and online harm*. Routledge.

Kranzberg, M. (1986). Technology and history: Kranzberg's laws. *Technology and Culture*, 27(3), 544–560.

Nutt, D. (2020.) *Drink?:The new science of alcohol and your health*. Yellow Kite.

Prensky, M. (2001). Digital natives, digital immigrants. *On the Horizon*, 9(5), 1–6.

Seong, E. et al. (2021). Relationship of socials and behavioural characteristics to suicidality in community adolescents with self-harm. Considering contagion and connection on social media. *Frontiers in Psychology*, 12, 691438.

Twenge, J. (2020). Increase in depression, self-harm, and suicide among US adolescents after 2012 and links to technology use. Possible mechanisms. *Psychiatric Research in Clinical Practice*, 2(1), 19–25.

CHAPTER 2

Bennett-Levy, J., Butler, G., Fennel, M., Hackman, A., Mueller, M.,& Westbrook, D. (2004). *Oxford guide to behavioural experiments in cognitive therapy*. Oxford University Press.

Bowlby, J. (1997). *Attachment and loss* (2nd ed.). Pimlico.

Brennan, I., & Bahn, K. (1991) Door-in-the-face, that's-not-all, and legitimizing a paltry contribution: Reciprocity, contrast effect and social judgement theory explanations. *Advances in Communication Research*, 18, 586–590.

Centre for Humane Technology (n.d.) The social dilemma. www.humanetech.com.

Corr, P., & Plagnol, A. (2018). *Behavioural economics, the basics*. Routledge.

Csikszentmihalyi, M. (1992/2002) *Flow. The classic work on how to achieve happiness*. Rider.

Dana, D. (2018). *Polyvagal theory in therapy. Engaging the rhythm of regulation*. WW Norton and Co.

Fonagy, P. (2001). *Attachment theory and psychoanalysis*. Routledge.

Fortune, J. (2022). *Why we play. How to find joy and meaning in everyday life*. Thread Books.

Grigutsch, L., Lewe, G., Rothermund, K., & Koranyi, N. (2019). Implicit wanting without implicit liking: a test of incentive-sensitization theory in the context of smoking addiction using the wanting-implicit-association test (W-IAT). *Journal of Behaviour Therapy and Experimental Psychiatry*, 64, 9–14.

Haidt, J. (2019). *The coddling of the American mind. How good intentions and bad ideas are setting up a generation for failure*. Penguin.

Harris, T. (2016). *How technology is hijacking your mind*. https://medium.com/thrive-global/how-technology-hijacks-peoples-minds-from-a-magician-and-google-s-design-ethicist-56d62ef5edf3.

Heath, R. (2012). *Seducing the subconscious: the psychology of emotional influence in advertising*. Wiley.

Hillman, J., Fowlie, D., & MacDonald, T. (2023). Social verification theory: A new way to conceptualize validation, dissonance, and belonging. *Personality and Social Psychology Review*, 27(3), 309–331.

James, W. (2017). *The principles of psychology* (Vols 1–2; his works from 1890 revised in 1918). Pantianos Classics.

Knibbs, C. (2022a). *Bodies, brains and technology – The real social dilemma*. TEDx Doncaster. https://www.youtube.com/watch?v=lRX_DWo3KPs.

Knibbs, C. (2022b). *Children, technology and healthy development*. Routledge.

Kowert, R. (2021). Jargon Schmargon: Parasocial Relationships. Psychgeist Channel on YouTube. https://www.youtube.com/watch?v=Zjl2BFv0Z74.

Le Doux, J. (2015). *Anxious. The modern mind in the age of anxiety*. Oneworld.

Lieberman, D., & Long, M. (2019). *The molecule of more. How a single chemical in your brain drives, love sex, creativity, and will determine the fate of the human race*. Benbella Books.

Madigan, S., Browne, D., Racine, N., Mori, C., & Tough, S. (2019). Association between screen time and children's performance on a developmental screening test. *JAMA Pediatrics*, 173(3), 244–250.

Morin, C., & Renvoise, P. (2018). *The persuasion code. How neuromarketing can help you persuade anyone, anywhere, anytime*. Wiley.

Music, G. (2017). *Nurturing natures. Attachment and children's emotional, sociocultural and brain development* (2nd ed.). Routledge.

Nelson-Field, K. (2020). *The attention economy and how media works. Simple truths for marketers*. Palgrave Macmillan.

Porges, S. (2011). *The Polyvagal theory. Neurophysiological foundations of emotions attachment, communication and self-regulation*. WW Norton and Co.

Porges, S. (2021). *Polyvagal safety. Attachment, communication, self-regulation*. WW Norton and Co.

Seigel, D. (2012). *The pocket guide to interpersonal neurobiology. An integrative handbook of the mind*. WW Norton and Co.

Shotton, R. (2023). *The illusion of choice: 16 ½ psychological biases that influence what we buy*. Harriman.

Woolard, J. (2010). *Psychology for the classroom: Behaviourism*. Routledge.

CHAPTER 3

American Psychological Association (n.d.). APA reaffirms position on violent video games and violent behaviour. https://www.apa.org/news/press/releases/2020/03/violent-video-games-behavior.

Anderson, C., & Bushman, B. (2001). Effects of violent video games on aggressive behavior, aggressive cognition, aggressive affect, physiological arousal, and prosocial behavior: A meta-analytic review of the scientific literature. *Psychological Science*, 12, 353–359.

Anderson, C. A., & Bushman, B. J. (2018). Media violence and the general aggression model. *Journal of Social Issues*, 74(2), 386–413.

Ashton, H., Milliman, J., Telford, R., & Thompson, J. (1973). Stimulant and depressant effects of cigarette smoking on brain activity in man. *British Journal of Pharmacology*, 48(4), 715–717.

Bandura, A., Ross, D., & Ross, S. A. (1961). Transmission of aggression through imitation of aggressive models. *The Journal of Abnormal and Social Psychology*, 63(3), 575.

Barrett, L. Feldman (2018). *How emotions are made. The secret life of the brain*. Pan Books.

Berne, E. (1964). *Games people play. The psychology of human relationships*. Penguin.

Boccamazzo, R., & Kowert, R. (2020). Video game addiction. What do know now? https://www.takethis.org/2019/10/video-game-addiction-what-do-we-know-now/.

Bradway, K., & McCoard, B. (1997). *Sandplay: Silent workshop of the psyche*. Routledge.

Ferguson, C. (2010). Blazing angels or resident evil? Can violent video games be a force for good? *Review of General Psychology*, 14, 68–81.

Griffiths, M. (2020). A brief overview of loot boxes in video gaming. In Kowert, R., & Quandt, T. *The video game debate 2. Revisiting the physical, social, and psychological effects of video games* (Chapter 2). Routledge.

Gross, J. (1998). The emerging field of emotion regulation: An integrative review. *Review of General Psychology*, 2(3), 271–299.

Guidi, J., Lucente, M., Sonino, N., & Fava, G. (2020). Allostatic load and its impact on health: A systematic review. *Psychotherapy and Psychosomatics*, 90, 11–27.

Kirsh, S., Olczak, P., & Mounts, J. (2005). Violent video games induce an affect processing bias. *Media Psychology*, 7, 239–250.

Knibbs, C. (2023). *Children, technology and healthy development*. Routledge.

Kowert, R., & Quandt, T. (2020). *The video game debate 2. Revisiting the physical, social, and psychological effects of video games*. Routledge.

Langman, P. (2009). Rampage school shooters: A typology. *Aggression and Violent Behavior*, 14, 79–86.

Markey, P., & Ferguson, C. (2017). *Mortal combat. Why the war on violent video games is wrong*. BenBella Books.

Marrodan, J., & Moraga, R. (2024). *Sandtray applications to trauma therapy*. Routledge.

Oaklander, V. (1978). *Windows to our children: A gestalt therapy approach to children and adolescents*. Gestalt Journal Press.

Orme, S. (2020). Playing to win. In Kowert, R., & Quandt, T. *The video game debate 2. Revisiting the physical, social, and psychological effects of video games* (Chapter 6). Routledge.

Owen, N., Salmon, J., Koohsari, M., Turrell, G., & Giles-Corti, B. (2014). Sedentary behaviour and health: mapping environmental and social contexts to underpin chronic disease prevention. *British Journal of Sports Medicine*, 48, 174–177.

Peng, W., & Liu, M. (2010). Online gaming dependency: A preliminary study in China. *Cyberpsychology Behaviour in Social Networking*, 13(3), 329–333.

Przybylski, A., & Weinstein, N. (2019). Violent video game engagement is not associated with adolescents aggressive behaviour. Evidence from a registered report. *Royal Society Open Science*, 6(2).

Stephens-Davidowitz, S. (2018). *Everybody lies: What the internet can tell us about who we really are*. Bloomsbury.

Williams, D., & Skoric, M. (2005). Internet fantasy violence: A test of aggression in an online game. *Communication Monographs*, 72, 217–233.

World Health Organization. (2022). ICD-11: International classification of diseases (11th revision). https://icd.who.int/.

CHAPTER 4

American Psychiatric Association (APA). (2013). *Diagnostic and statistical manual of mental disorders* (5th ed.). American Psychiatric Association.

Asch, S. E. (1951). Effects of group pressure upon the modification and distortion. In H. Guetzkow (ed), *Groups, leadership and men; research in human relations* (pp. 177–190). Carnegie Press.

Baddeley, A. (1997). *Working memory*. Clarendon Press.

Baddeley, A., Thompson, N., & Buchannan, M. (1975). Word length and the structure of short term memory. *Journal of Verbal Learning and Verbal Behaviour*, 14, 575–589.

Berne, E. (1964). *Games people play. The psychology of human relationships*. Penguin.

Britton, E. (2015). Talking to your doctor. https://joinclubsoda.com/hub/talking-your-doctor-part-i/.

Brunner, R., Parzer, P., Haffner J., Steen, R., Roos, J., Klett, M., & Resch, F. (2007). Prevalence and psychological correlates of occasional and repetitive deliberate self-harm in adolescents. *Archives of Pediatrics & Adolescent Medicine*, 161(7), 641–649.

Bryman, A. (2001). *Social research methods*. Oxford University Press.

Centre for Humane Technology (n.d.) www.humanetech.com.

Cook, D. (2001). Exchange value as pedagogy in children's leisure: Moral panics in children's culture at century's end. *Leisure Sciences*, 23, 81–98.

Hanson, R. (2013). *Hardwiring happiness: The practical science of reshaping your brain and your life*. Rider Publications.

Haidt, J. (2019) *The coddling of the American mind. How good intentions and bad ideas are setting up a generation for failure*. Penguin.

Heath, A. (2023). Marck Zuckerberg is ready to fight Elon Musk in a cage fight. https://www.theverge.com/2023/6/21/23769263/mark-zuckerberg-elon-musk-fight-cage-match-worldstar.

Huberman, A. (2023). Huberman lab podcast. https://www.hubermanlab.com/podcast.

Huesmann, L., & Eron, L. (1986). *Television and the aggressive child: A cross-national comparison*. Hillsdale.

Huesmann, L., Moise-Titus J., Podolski, C., & Eron, L. (2003). Longitudinal relations between children's exposure to TV violence and their aggressive and violent behavior in young adulthood: 1977–1992. *Developmental Psychology*, 39(2), 201–221.

Internet World Stats (2021). Usage and population data. 5 billion connections. https://www.internetworldstats.com/stats.htm and https://datareportal.com/global-digital-overview.

Jamieson, D. (2010). *Mint condition: How baseball cards became an American obsession*. Grove Press.

Jones, D., & Podolsky, S. (2015) The history and fate of the gold standard. https://www.thelancet.com/journals/lancet/article/PIIS0140-6736(15)60742-5/fulltext.

Kelly, Y., Zilanawala, A., Booker, C., & Sacker A. (2018). Social media use and adolescent mental health: Findings from the UK Millennium Cohort Study. *EClinicalMedicine*, 6, 59–68.

Kinsey, A. C. et al. (1948/1998). *Sexual behavior in the human male*. Indiana University Press.

Knibbs, C. (2022). *Bodies, brains and technology – The real social dilemma*. TEDx Doncaster. https://www.youtube.com/watch?v=lRX_DWo3KPs.

Knibbs, C. (2023a). *Children technology and healthy development*. Routledge. https://www.youtube.com/watch?v=lRX_DWo3KPs.

Knibbs, C. (2023b). Self-Harm. In *Online harms and cybertrauma* (Chapter 7). Routledge.

Logie, R. (1995). *Visio-spatial working memory*. Psychology Press.

Lomas, N. (2104). Yo the one-word messaging app, updates so it's no quite so absurdly simple anymore. TechCrunch. A https://techcrunch.com/2014/08/12/yo-grows-up/.

Lopes L., Valentini, J., Monteiro, T., Costacurta, M., Soares, L., Telfar-Barnard, L., & Nunes, P. (2022). Problematic social media use and its relationship with depression or anxiety: A systematic review. *Cyberpsychology Behaviour in Social Networking*, 25(11), 691–702.

Madigan, S., Browne, D., Racine, N., Mori, C., & Tough, S. (2019). Association between screen time and children's performance on a developmental screening test. *JAMA Pediatrics*, 173(3), 244–250.

Malecki, S., Quinn, K., Zilbert, N., Razak, F., Ginsburg, S., Verma, A., & Melvin, L. (2019). Understanding the use and perceived impact of a medical podcast: Qualitative study. *JMIR Medical Education*, 5.

Markey, P., Ivory, J., Slotter, E., Oliver, M., & Maglalang, O. (2019). He does not look like video games made him do it: Racial stereotypes and school shootings. *Psychology of Popular Media Culture*, 9(4), 493–498.

Memon, A., Sharma, S., Mohite, S., & Jain, S. (2018). The role of online social networking on deliberate self-harm and suicidality in adolescents: A systematized review of literature. *Indian Journal of Psychiatry*, 60, 384–392.

Milgram, S. (1963). Behavioral study of obedience. *The Journal of Abnormal and Social Psychology*, 67(4), 371–378.

Miller, J., Mills, K., Vuorre, M., Orben, A. & Przybylski, A. (2023) Impact of digital screen media activity on functional brain organization in late childhood: Evidence from the ABCD study. *Cortex*, 169, 290–308.

Murray J. (1973). Television and violence: Implications of the Surgeon General's research program. *American Psychologist*, 28, 472–478.

Murthy, V. (2023). Social media and youth mental health: The U.S. Surgeon General's advisory. https://www.usphs.gov/.

Nutt, D. (2009). Equasy: An overlooked addiction with implications for the current debate on drug harms. *Journal of Psychopharmacology*, 23, 3–5.

Ogunlade, J. (1979). Personality Characteristics Related to Susceptibility to Behavioral Contagion. *Social Behavior and Personality*, 7, 205–208.

Orben A., & Przybylski A. (2019). The association between adolescent well-being and digital technology use. *Nature Human Behaviour*, 3(2), 173–182.

Perez, S. (2014). Yo has spawned an army of clones. TechCrunch. https://techcrunch.com/gallery/yo-has-spawned-an-army-of-clones/.

Royal Meteorological Society (2021) Weather, climate and chaos theory. https://www.metlink.org/blog/weather-climate-and-chaos-theory/.

Sharifian, N., & Zahodne, L. (2020). Social media bytes: Daily associations between social media use and everyday memory failures across the adult life span. *The Journals of Gerontology Series*, 75(3), 540–548.

Shrier, A. (2021). *Irreversible damage, teenage girls and the transgender craze*. Swift Press.

Shugerman, E. (2023). Meet the Huberman husbands. https://www.thedailybeast.com/meet-the-andrew-huberman-husbands-and-their-long-suffering-wives.

Siegel, D. (2014). *Brainstorm. The power and purpose of the teenage brain*. Jeremy P Tarcher.

Tuckute, G., Paunov, A., Small, H., Mineroff, Z., Blank, I., & Fedorenko, E. (2022). Frontal language areas do not emerge in the absence of temporal language areas: A case study of an individual born without a left temporal lobe. *Neuropsycholgia*, 169.

Twenge, J. (2017). Have smartphones destroyed a generation? *The Atlantic*. https://www.theatlantic.com/magazine/archive/2017/09/has-the-smartphone-destroyed-a-generation/534198/.

Twenge, J. (2023). *Generations: the real differences between Gen Z, millenials, Gen X boomers and silents and what they mean for America's future*. Atria Books.

Twenge J., Joiner, T., Rogers, M., & Martin, G. (2018). Increases in depressive symptoms, suicide-related outcomes, and suicide rates among U.S. adolescents after 2010 and links to increased new media screen time. *Clinical Psychological Science*, 6, 3–17.

van Geel, M., Vedder, P., & Tanilon, J. (2104). Relationship between peer victimization, cyberbullying, and suicide in children and adolescents: A meta-analysis. *JAMA Pediatrics*, 168(5), 435–442.

Waltz, E. (2018). Wearable brain scanners. https://spectrum.ieee.org/a-new-wearable-brain-scanner.

World Health Organization. (2022). *ICD-11: International classification of diseases* (11th revision). https://icd.who.int/.

Zimbardo, P. (1973). On the ethics of intervention in human psychological research: With special reference to the Stanford Prison Experiment. *Cognition*, 2(2), 243–256.

CHAPTER 5

American Psychiatric Association (APA). (2013). *Diagnostic and statistical manual of mental disorders* (5th ed.). American Psychiatric Association.

Berne, E. (1964). *Games people play. The psychology of human relationships*. Penguin.

Bowlby, J. (1997). *Attachment and loss* (2nd ed.). Pimlico.

Clear, J. (2018). *Atomic habits. An easy and proven way to build good habits and break bad ones*. Random House.

Felitti, V., Anda, R., Nordenberg, D., Williamson, D., Spitz, A., Edwards, V., Koss, M., & Marks, J. (1998). Relationship of childhood abuse and household dysfunction to many of the leading causes of death in adults. The Adverse Childhood Experiences (ACE) Study. *American Journal of Preventative Medicine*, 14(4), 245–258.

Harris, S. (2015). *Waking up. Searching for spirituality without religion*. Black Swan.

Heinrich, L. & Gullone, E. (2006). The clinical significance of loneliness: a literature review. *Clinical Psychology Review*, 26(6), 695–718.

Kaufman, S. B. (2020). *Transcend. The new science of self-actualization*. Tarcherperigree.

Knibbs, C. (2022). *Bodies, brains and technology – The real social dilemma*. TEDx Doncaster. https://www.youtube.com/watch?v=lRX_DWo3KPs.

Knibbs, C. (2023). *Children technology and healthy development*. Routledge. https://www.youtube.com/watch?v=lRX_DWo3KPs.

Maslow, A. H. (1943). A theory of human motivation. *Psychological Review*, 50(4), 370–396.

Panda, S. (2018). *The Circadian code*. Penguin Random House.

Siegel, D. (2016). *Mind: A journey to the heart of being human*. WW Norton and Co.

Siegel, D. (2019). Presence, parenting and the planet. Talks at Google. https://www.youtube.com/watch?v=Ouzb_Urt7LQ IN.

Sternberg, R. (2008). *The new psychology of love*. Yale University Press.

Walker, M. (2018). Why we sleep. The new science of sleep and dreams. Penguin.

World Health Organization. (2022). *ICD-11: International classification of diseases* (11th revision). https://icd.who.int/.

CHAPTER 6

Baker, P., & Norton, L. (2019). *Fat loss forever*. Amazon print on demand.

Bowlby, J. (1997). *Attachment and loss* (2nd ed.). Pimlico.

Çekici, H., & Sanlier, N. (2017). Current nutritional approaches in managing autism spectrum disorder: A review. *Nutritional Neuroscience*, 22, 145–155.

Donaldson, J. (2016). *The Gruffalo*. Macmillan Children's Books.

Edwards, D. (2021). *My first animal moves: A Children's book to encourage kids and their parents to move more, sit less and decrease screen time*. Explore Publishing.

Farello, G., Altieri, C., Cutini, M., Pozzobon, G., & Verrotti, A. (2019). Review of the literature on current changes in the timing of pubertal development and the incomplete forms of early puberty. *Frontiers in Pediatrics*, 7.

Heitman, K. et al. (2023). Snacks contribute considerably to total dietary intakes among adults stratified by glycemia in the United States. *PLOS Glob Public Health*, 3(10).

Huberman, A. (2023). Huberman lab podcast. https://www.hubermanlab.com/podcast.

Knibbs, C. (2022). *Children, technology and healthy development*. Routledge.

Knibbs, C. (2023a). *Children and sexual based online harms*. Routledge.

Knibbs, C. (2023b). *Cybertrauma and online harm*. Routledge.

Naidoo, U. (2020). *The food mood connection*. Short Books.

Palmer, C. (2023). *Brain Energy. A revolutionary breakthrough in understanding mental health – and improving treatment for anxiety, depression, OCD, PTSD, and more*. Benbella Books.

Robinson, K. (2007). Do schools kill creativity? TED talk. https://www.youtube.com/watch?v=iG9CE55wbtY.

Siegel, D. (1999/2020). *The developing mind* (3rd ed.). The Guildford Press

Siegel, D. (2010). *The mindful therapist. A clinician's guide to mindsight and neural integration*. WW Norton and Co.

Siegel, D. (2014). *Brainstorm. The power and purpose of the teenage brain*. Jeremy P Tarcher.

Walker, M. (2018). *Why we sleep. The new science of sleep and dreams*. Penguin.

CHAPTER 7

Allen, K. (2021). *The Psychology of belonging*. Routledge.

Anthony, K., & Nagel, D. M. (2010). *Therapy online: A practical guide*. Sage.

Bean, A. (2018). *Working with video gamers and games in therapy. A clinician's guide*. Routledge.

Berne, E. (1964). *Games people play. The psychology of human relationships*. Penguin.

Csikszentmihalyi, M. (1992/2002). *Flow. The classic work on how to achieve happiness*. Rider.

Duckworth, A. (2017) Grit: Why passion and resilience are the secrets to success. Vermillion.

Goodyear-Brown, P. (2019). *Trauma and play therapy: Helping children heal*. Routledge.

Heinrich, L., & Gullone, E. (2006). The clinical significance of loneliness: A literature review. *Clinical Psychology Review*, 26(6), 695–718.

Kaye, L. (2017). *What your emoji says about you*. TEDx Vienna. https://www.youtube.com/watch?v=5hiQB0kqIsY.

Knibbs, C. (2016). *Cybertrauma: the darker side of the internet for children and young people*. Kindle book.

Knibbs, C. (2022a). *Children, technology and healthy development*. Routledge.

Knibbs, C. (2022b). *Bodies, brains and technology – The real social dilemma*. TEDx Doncaster. https://www.youtube.com/watch?v=lRX_DWo3KPs.

Kowert, R. (2016). *A parent's guide to video games*. CreateSpace Independent.

Kotler, S. (2021). *The art of impossible. A peak performance primer*. Harper.

Kotler, S., & Wheal, J. (2018). *Stealing fire: How Silicon Valley, the Navy SEALs, and maverick scientists are revolutionizing the way we live and work*. Dey Street Books.

Kuhn, K. (2022). The constant mirror: Self-view and attitudes to virtual meetings. *Computer Human Behavior*, 128, 1–7.

McGonigal, J. (2015). *Superbetter a revolutionary approach to getting stronger, happier, braver and more resilient*. Viking Books.

Schalkwyk, G., Marin, C., Ortiz, M., Rolison, M., Qayyum, Z., McPartland, J., Lebowitz, E., Siegel, D. (2022). *Intraconnected: Mwe as the integration of belonging and identity*. WW Norton and Co.

Turkle, S. (2015). *Reclaiming conversation. The power of talk in a digital age*. Penguin.

Volkmar, F., & Silverman, W. (2017). Social media use, friendship quality, and the moderating role of anxiety in adolescents with Autism Spectrum Disorder. *Journal of Autism and Developmental Disorders*, 47, 2805–2813.

Wheal, J. (2021). *Recapture the rapture. Rethinking God, sex, and death in a world that's lost its mind*. Harper Collins.

CHAPTER 8

Barrett, L. Feldman (2018). *How emotions are made. The secret life of the brain*. Pan Books.

Barrett, L. Feldman, Lewis, M., & Haviland-Jones, J. (2016). *The Handbook of Emotions* (4th ed.). Guildford Press.

Brewer, J. (2018). *The craving mind: From cigarettes to smartphones to love –Why we get hooked and how we can break bad habits*. Yale University Press.

Clear, J. (2018). *Atomic habits. An easy and proven way to build good habits and break bad ones*. Random House.

de Botton, A. (2023). *A therapeutic journey: Lessons from the school of life*. Penguin.

Dweck, C. (2017). *Mindset: Changing the way you think to fulfil your potential* (6th ed.). Robinson.

Eckman, P. (2004). *Emotions revealed: Understanding faces and feelings*. Phoenix.

Eyal, N. (2014). *Hooked: How to build habit forming products*. Penguin.

Eyal, N. (2020). *Indistractable: How to control your attention and choose your life*. Bloomsbury.

Gazzelay, A., & Rosen, L. (2016). *A distracted mind. Ancient brains in a technological world*. MIT Press.

Glei, J. (2016). *Unsubscribe how to kill email anxiety, avoid distractions and get REAL work done*. Piatkus.

Goleman, D. (1995). *Emotional intelligence*. Bloomsbury.

Goleman, D., & Davidson, R. (2018.) *The science of meditation: How to change your brain, mind and body*. Penguin.

Hanh, T. (2008). *The miracle of mindfulness: The classic guide to meditation by the world's most revered master*. Rider.

Koutsoklenis, A., & Honkasilta, J. (2023). ADHD in the DSM-5-TR: What has changed and what has not. *Frontiers in Psychiatry*, 10(13).

Mann D. (2020). *Gestalt therapy: 100 key points and techniques* (2nd ed.). Routledge.

Newport, C. (2019). *Digital minimalism: Choosing a focused life in a noisy world*. Penguin.

Planton, S., Jucla, M., Roux, F., & Démonet, J. (2013). The 'handwriting brain': A meta-analysis of neuroimaging studies of motor versus orthographic processes. *Cortex*, 49, 2772–2787.

Ullrich, P., & Lutgendorf, S. (2002). Journaling about stressful events: Effects of cognitive processing and emotional expression. *Annals of Behavioral Medicine*, 24, 244–250.

Williams, M., & Penman, D. (2011). *Mindfulness, a practical guide to finding peace in a frantic world*. Piakuts Books.

GLOSSARY

Algorithm: a computer program that is specially aimed at identification and pattern recognition of the 'inputs' it receives and is often used to measure the interactions of users on specific websites, platforms, or on social media sites. This is often then used to drive specific patterns to the users based on their previous interactions.

Artificial Intelligence: it is suggested this is the 'evolving intelligence' of the machine programmed to learn and think like a human. Many of these programs/algorithms are based on large numbers of transformers (no, not the robots in the cartoons or films) and can also be called large language models (LLMs).

It is also a discipline of study, a name for machines or robots with sentient-like characteristics that use computer driven learning (such as those in films like: The Terminator, iRobot) and a term coined by Alan Turing to assess whether a computer could 'outsmart' a human into believing it was human (these are not accurate academic definitions but laid out for the reader to understand). This is not quite the same as machine learning or intelligence and often these terms can be over inflated or confused with AI. There are now many forms of this public facing AI 'model' on the market that people can use, and many AI programs have been in use for many years on the back end of websites and social media platforms driving what we interact with such as shopping recommendations.

Attention economics: a discipline devoted to measuring, manipulating, and creating more attentional material or the/an experience that 'taps into' attentional processes. How big tech and algorithms find, measure and utilises those patterns of attention = more time on 'this' platform.

Behavioural economics: like attentional versions this discipline is focused upon treating humans like skinner pigeons and rats (the animals used by B. F. Skinner) and creating specific behaviours based on innate drives such as attention and fear. A manipulation of humans under the guise of 'ethical behaviourism'.

Contact hunger: a term created by Eric Berne (1964) to describe the innate drive and 'urge' to be in contact with people so you can receive a stroke of recognition (sometimes called recognition hunger).

Cyber ethics: a discipline of ethics relating to how technology is applied, utilised, or interacted with by human beings and how that interface of technology and person requires distinct thinking about safety for humans.

Desktop device: often kept on, under, or next to a desk; it often means a personal home computer.

Drug: a substance usually injected, ingested, or inhaled into the body causing physiological and psychological changes to the person. This includes legal prescription medication and illegal or illicit substances.

FOMO: fear of missing out, which is a human emotion. Overused ion the space of technology media articles and by pop-psychologists who don't understand why someone might feel this (but clickbait acronyms sell).

Gamer: a term used to identify gaming 'people' though there is no specific definition as to how much or how often gaming time one needs to engage in to be able to use this identity (it is far too nebulous to identify a gamer by phenotype, genotype, or any other criterion).

Gamification: the intentional process applied to a task to create the illusion of a game, by creating an outcome that is achievable in small steps.

Gaming: a term normally used to denote playing a computer or video games (and sometimes mobile types too). Not usually used for anyone playing kerplunk, snap, or cribbage. Could be used for table top role playing games (TTRPG) such as Warhammer or Dungeons and Dragons; can be used positively and negatively.

Handheld device: a device that a user interacts with that can be held by one or two hands, for example a smartphone or tablet.

Haptic technology: a form of tech, often worn close to the body such as gloves, vests, or suits that provide the wearer with feedback directly as a touch sensation.

iWant: the new name for pester power related to tech wants (another tongue in cheek play on words).

Mal-information: the exacerbation (stretching) of the 'truth' so to speak so that things that are communicated are not false, but misrepresented to be 'truer' than they are. For example 'sugarless' drinks can contain sugar, as long as it's under five calories. Yes really.

Media: a term used to denote text, audio, and visual images that are accessible on platforms, apps, websites, and online. Also refers to videos, cinema, TV, and the industry which produces or reports on this material (e.g. main stream media)

NEAT: non-exercise active thermogenesis: the movements you make during the day that are not classified as intentional exercise.

Olympic addiction disorder: sadly a gold, silver, or bronze medallist dysfunction where in an attempt to achieve the prestige status, the Olympian engages in excessive practice to the detriment of many other processes in their life. This consumes them on a daily basis and affects dreams and conversations and often results in a co-addict-facilitation in the form of a coach who presses them to continue their 'regime', for their own good, and so they reach the 'top spot' (tongue-in-cheek-disorder here and NOT REAL).

Platform: a term used to denote a space (often social media) that many users can visit and interact with other users on/in or through.

Randomised control trial: the Olympic standard of research studies (or so it is said). Research is conducted with neither the 'researcher' carrying out the tests or the 'participants' knowing what is being tested or in which group (randomly allocated hence the name) and therefore preventing biases/influence over the results. Both are said to be blind to the research 'hypothesis' and often used in research with such a hypothesis (but not usually used in qualitative studies such as the social sciences).

SATs: Standard Assessment Tests taken by children in Year 6 of primary schools in the UK (aged 10 to 11).

Screentime: a term that has been used to mean time on devices and or smartphones. Does not include TV/cinema or videos before the internet and has become synonymous with 'time online', 'time gaming' and is a term often used to explain how we can measure our interactions on devices. It has been applied by large tech companies to be seen to be doing something to help you manage this 'screentime'. Now a measurement on some smart devices which equates to little else other than time spent on apps (so you can berate, punish yourself or others or rejoice in the little amount of time you use this particular device).

Social contagion (online): a proposition that emotions, resulting in specific behaviours, are now a part of the social media experience – this is outside of the first introduction of this terminology where it related to groups of people often in a corporeal setting.

Social media: a very broad term used to denote any platform, application or program where 'users' can socialise in some way.

Violent video games: see the section on this description as this is a vague concept and even cartoon style games can involve violence (and aggression, and power and other aspects associated with violent behaviour)

Zoom fatigue: a term to denote the tired feeling after many (endless) video meetings.

Printed in the United States
by Baker & Taylor Publisher Services